My Story, His Glory

HIS FAITHFULNESS IN MY DARKNESS

MY STORY, HIS GLORY:
HIS FAITHFULNESS IN MY DARKNESS

Printed in the United States of America

ISBN
Paperback: 979-8-3304-6650-4

Photos by Saving Grace
Edited by Lori Loomis
Proofread by Brynn Sowers
Book design by Jay Esteban and AM Hernandez
Promotional video by Ronald Biyo

My Story, His Glory

HIS FAITHFULNESS IN MY DARKNESS

Saving Grace

INTRODUCTION

I'm just your average small-town girl from North Carolina, small town as in everybody knows everybody . . . and their business. I had loving parents who only wanted better for me and my sister than they themselves had growing up.

I enjoyed spring nights on a softball field, and winter was designated to a basketball court. We loved camping and boating on Jordan Lake through the summers, and the fall wasn't complete without a backyard bonfire and s'mores. I still remember riding my bike with my cousins in the trailer park, wind in our hair and not a care in the world.

Friday nights were spent at "Wheels," our local skating rink, while Saturdays were spent making mud pies with friends and singing a little ditty 'bout Jack and Diane to the top of our lungs. Sundays, one way or the other, had us in a pew singing "Amazing Grace" before I even understood the depth of what grace truly was.

Yeah, those were the good old days alright. But it was the spring of '98 when everything changed.

TABLE OF CONTENTS

Where It All Began

This is my story, this is my song,
praising my Savior, all the day long.

Something about spring just breathes new life into you. I loved waking up to the windows open, the crisp morning breeze, and birds singing a new melody. It is truly one of my favorite things.

I had only one sister, and she was two years older than me. We were polar opposites of each other. With her long, golden blonde hair, baby blue eyes, long legs, and perfect figure, everyone deemed her to be a model. Me, on the other hand . . . well, I was rather compared to one such as Raggedy Ann. I was the tomboy who'd rather be outside than in and shooting layups rather than laying out working on my tan. I was the black sheep of my family.

Our biggest battle was fighting for time in the bathroom. While she needed forty-five minutes to put on her makeup and whatever else it took to look so perfect, I simply begged for a corner of the sink just so I could brush my teeth.

"ACHOO!" She let out a sneeze so abruptly, and man were her sneezes ever so obnoxiously loud, but they'd make me laugh after the initial startle. "God bless you," I said. Before I could even start to giggle, I found myself pinned against the bathroom wall. The molding pressed into my back, my mind racing, unable to understand what was happening.

"Don't ever say HIS name around me again, EVER!" my sister demanded before she let me loose and walked out of the bathroom without another word.

My world fell silent. I heard nothing but the echoes of her words. It was as if I lost all mobility of my body as I stood frozen in front of the mirror. Was I even breathing? I felt my tears begin to form, and something within my soul knew life would never be the same.

I composed myself, wiped my tears, and as usual, put a smile on my face because that's what we do in this family. What happens in this house stays in this house. I got on the bus and headed off to school, and it seemed that it was just some freak accident. Perhaps I had just imagined the incident in the bathroom. My sister was all smiles as we parted ways, as though a spiritual war didn't just break out twenty-two minutes ago back at the house.

My life seemed to go on as normal for quite some time, but I often found myself pondering what happened in the bathroom that morning. We went to church every Sunday morning, Sunday night, and even Wednesday night. Yep, we were 100 percent born and bred Southern Baptist. So why all of a sudden could she not stand to hear the mention of His name? It shook me. It birthed a fear of my sister, and the worst part of it all, I couldn't share it with anyone.

Summer came and like every other year, we planned our family vacation at Myrtle Beach. My dad and I would burn to a crisp, despite the hourly rebathing in sunscreen. Meanwhile, my mom and sister would just tan perfectly.

None of it seemed to matter that summer. I felt like what happened in the bathroom that spring morning was behind us and life was back to normal. Camping at Jordan Lake, ghost stories by the fire, s'mores in my hair . . . it never failed to happen. We had a good life—a blessed life.

We spent nights at my grandmother's down at "Ronnie Johnson's Trailer Park," and I swear it felt like our whole family lived there at one time. Those were the best nights, cackling into the midnight hours with my cousins. Those were indeed the "good old days."

Fall rolled around, and school was getting back into full swing. It wasn't long before I started seeing an old familiar side of my sister I prayed I'd never see again. I found myself walking on eggshells when she would come around, and I just prayed to stay under her radar. She didn't have to say or do anything; it was as though fear became a tangible being.

It wasn't always like this. Not at all. Honestly, I believe that's what fed the fear inside of me. I never knew which sister I would be speaking to. As winter crept upon us, it's as though her heart grew colder. There was so much anger, and I could never understand why.

To me, there seemed to be no reason for it, almost as though she was living a life none of us knew about.

I remember being outside under the old pecan tree. This tree produced hundreds of pecans every year; it was massive! It's where our driveway extended and where my dad put an in-ground basketball goal up for me. He built a barn with my uncle and his cousin and installed floodlights on the outside of it just above the door so we could play late into the night. He was so proud of that barn. He would spend hours out there just "piddling around"—as he called it—while I practiced my jump shot. He was my best friend at eleven years old.

We even built a large fenced-in area for our shepherd dogs to roam and play. It was part of our chores to feed them and keep their pen clean. I still ride past that old house, and though it looks so much different now, I still see my dad's blue pickup truck in the driveway with his boat attached and that old barn barely standing. Yet, there's still a light on my court, and I try to remember the best of times spent there before everything changed.

All Downhill from Here

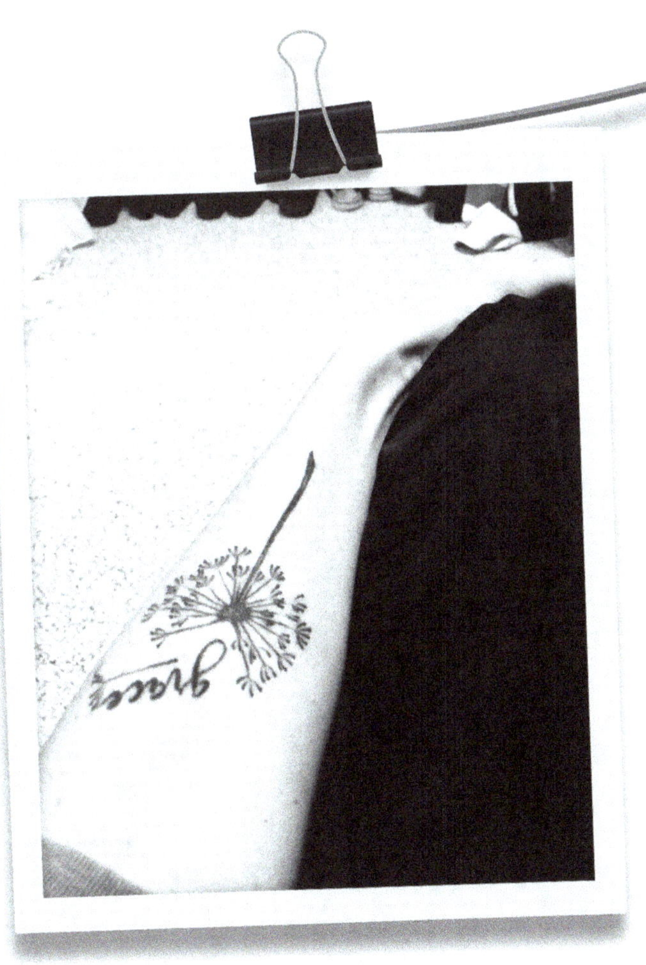

It was all fun and games until someone got hurt. I should have suspected something when she came out wanting to help me practice.

I watched as my ball rolled down the driveway toward the side door of our home where I saw my sister coming out. "Hey! Can you throw that back?" I asked. She replied, "I sure can" with a smirk on her face. She rushed toward me throwing the ball at my face with a greater agenda in mind. I shielded my face with my hands, unable to catch the ball from the force of the throw. I laughed it off as sibling rivalry.

She took a few more shots at me, and suddenly I was reminded of that morning in the bathroom. I felt the fear creeping back in, excavating at my very core. It was different this time. I saw it in her eyes. Her once baby blue eyes now looked more like a storm brewing. None of us would be ready for the hell she had already begun unleashing.

We lived sheltered lives. Dare I say even gullible? I remembered the first time my sister was excited to go to my grandmother's house. Even my parents were caught off guard. While I wanted to spend every weekend there with her, playing video games on the Nintendo (heck yes, my grandma was just that cool), my sister wanted nothing to do with her.

It wasn't long after we arrived that my sister grabbed the phone and pulled me down the hallway into the furthest bedroom of the trailer with her. I assumed she had her first boyfriend; afterall, she was in the eighth grade and I was now a sixth grader.

She closed the door quietly and locked us in. I questioned why she was acting so weird, but before I could question anything more, she said, "shut up and do exactly what I tell you to." She then instructed me to call her teacher, and if his wife answered the phone, just tell her that I am a student and I have a question about my homework.

"Ummm why, he's not my teacher and I don't have any home-work. This is just weird!" I turned to leave the room, but she pulled me back, shoving me on the bed. She grabbed my arm and proceeded to give me what we would call an Indian burn. In case you don't know, it is taking one's arm with both hands, twisting your hands in opposite directions, creating a burning sensation and leaving the arm red as though it had been burned.

"JUST DO IT!" she demanded. She threatened to tell our parents all sorts of lies, forcing me to succumb to her demands. Then I saw it. The darkness in her eyes had deepened, and I could no longer just shake off the fear as I did before.

She dialed the number and pressed the phone against my ear. Indeed it was a female that answered the phone.

With my sister pinning me against the wall, the phone pressed against my ear, and her eyes threatening me to utter a word different than the script she had given, I felt hopeless for the first time in my life.

"Yes ma'am, is Mr. Jones available? I am a student and have a question about our homework." Regrettably, I muttered through my sister's script, but the fear of her was consuming me the longer she kept me pinned against the wall.

She unlocked the door as she heard the lady calling for Mr. Jones through the phone. As soon as I heard the bass in his voice over the phone, I was thrown out of the room and she locked the door behind me.

I just stood in the hallway, wondering what I would say to my grandmother in the other room. How would I explain the red "burn marks" on my arm? As afraid as I was, unsure of what the future would entail for me, I was more afraid to not protect my sister.

I was thankful my grandma was consumed with conquering the next level in Super Mario Bros and was completely unaware of what had taken place in the back bedroom.

Don't you do it. Don't you judge my grandma! She was a good one—different sure, but she loved us and we knew it.

That was the first of many calls to Mr. Jones that happened that year. I was thankful I didn't have to see him at my school.

September 1999, a brand new school opened in our area, and for our small town, it was a big deal! I was so excited to be one of the first to walk the halls. Each grade had its own hallway, and we claimed it with great pride! I was entering as a seventh grader, so it was a little less daunting starting a new school and bringing two rival towns under one roof for the first time.

I worked hard and made sure I made the basketball team. While my home life was a nightmare no one could have ever fathomed, I found my joy on the court. We became undefeated champions our first year in that school, and I had never been so proud.

Yet, at home, I lived a life of fear, shame, and confusion. The phone calls to Mr. Jones continued, and the verbal threats became physical over time. Looking back now, I can only imagine the weight my sister carried. A weight like that would break anyone and unfortunately, it found its way to break our family.

Mr. Jones also became a part of this new establishment. I thought I would be okay. After all, our hallways were separated. I was safe from awkward encounters, for now. I was placed in a remedial reading class, which was being taken over by a substitute teacher. Ms. Lee was a God-fearing black woman that didn't take any crap. Don't get me wrong, she was fun and intentional about connecting with her students. She led the classroom with excellence and compassion for everyone under her care.

I'll never forget the day she saw me. I left her class and made my way back to the seventh-grade hallway. The hallways were full of students and teachers as the exchange of classes was taking place.

Before I knew it, I was standing beside none other than Mr. Jones. While I never knew what was said between him and my sister on phone calls . . . I knew whatever it was, was wrong. He wrapped his arm around me and hugged me, and I felt a piece of myself die from the inside out.

The abuse I was enduring at home from my sister was now creeping into my safe haven and escalating to a level I could not even begin to comprehend. I froze. I didn't know what to do. I had to protect my sister's secret or I knew there'd be even worse consequences when we got home.

Ms. Lee quickly pulled me from the pit I felt my soul plummeting into. All I remember her saying is, "You stay with me, I'll be walking you to your next class. You're mine." At the time, I didn't know if "you're mine" was a good thing or not. It didn't take long to realize that Ms. Lee was truly a Godsend, my protector. She saw me, and while we never spoke of the hell I was enduring at home, she made sure that I had a safe haven somewhere—even if it had been confined to just a classroom.

She was just the first of many teachers that God handpicked, knowing which ones would truly see me and protect me without knowing my story. Ms. Lee was just the first of many that poured into my life and still does to this day. I was able to finish out my years at that school without having Mr. Jones as a teacher and him never putting his hands on me again.

Broken doors, holes in walls, bruised body, and drowning in fear. How could our parents not suspect the horror I was enduring? I have made myself believe that they so passionately wanted us to have the best life, far better than they could have ever dreamed, that their passion blinded them and silenced them from asking hard questions.

> **Our reality had become a living nightmare and no one had yet found the courage to dig deeper.**

Not yet anyway.

In 2001, I became a freshman, and I was in the same school as my sister. I was determined to find answers, and I had only two years to find all the missing pieces to this puzzle. Why had my sister become so angry? Why did she feel she had to turn on me rather than confide in me? What was the big secret?

I had so many questions, and while my focus should have been on surviving high school and focusing on my future, my life was now consumed with uncovering the biggest scandal that had been playing out for four years now.

As one would suspect, I was thrilled to get to my physical education class and see who my teacher was. I was completely stunned when I realized it was my fourth grade teacher and role model. She was everything I wanted to be: a coach, compassionate, kind, teacher, role model—she was loved.

There she was. I wondered if she would remember me from so long ago. Of course she did! That's part of what made her stand out from the rest—we were more than a number in a classroom; we all had a name and a story.

For a brief moment, my agenda suddenly changed, and I found myself standing in the hallway of my high school as my fourth-grade self. With her back in my life, there was a glimpse of hope for my future. It was another person God strategically placed in my life to protect me and begin healing my heart.

Unfortunately, once I left her classroom or the gym, my laser focus returned sharply to finding answers to questions I had been carrying for too long.

It was a big high school, but my sister never was where she was supposed to be. I could not find her. I would even "go to the bathroom" and sneak to her classes to see if she was in there. Not once did I ever find her in the class she was meant to be in, which just added to my running list of agonizing questions.

Her hatred grew for me more every day. She hated me so much she threatened to beat the hell out of me like never before if I even told people we were sisters.

Not only could I not find her at school, I began not finding her at home. We'd get off the bus together, start our homework, and sometime between doing homework and doing our chores, she would vanish. I checked her room, every mirror in the house as she became slightly more vain as the years progressed, the barn, the dog pen . . . nowhere. But she would always manage to reappear before my parents got home from work. Whatever was going on would not only impact our lives, but our community.

We began talking about abuse in health class, the different types of abuse and how to ask for help. Tears began to well in my eyes as I fought hard to hold them in. I tried to drown out the words my teacher was saying. I didn't want her to see me this way. I didn't want her to see me beaten and broken, hopeless and defeated.

This lesson lasted for about a week, and I had a feeling that my time to find the answers to my questions would run out a lot sooner than anticipated.

I went hard. I knew I wouldn't find her in her classes, so I went farther than ever. There was another building that was connected by a breezeway that was designated for extracurricular classes. In fact, I thought I had caught a glimpse of her golden blonde hair on the run toward the breezeway. I was so perplexed as I knew she did not leave the house wearing what she currently had on.

I was so close to the answers I had been longing for—for so many years. I lost all awareness of the people around me and sprinted after her, shoving aside anyone who got in my way. What was she hiding? What was down there? Was it all linked to the phone calls from years ago? I burst through the door leading to the breezeway, then pulled open the door that granted me entrance to the building where I knew my sister was now hiding. With so many eyes on me, I looked into every classroom.

The first teacher directed me to leave that section of the building and go back to my class, but it may have been the first time I ever ignored a person of authority. Despite their instructions, I continued busting through every class, calling her name. I knew with everything in me that I finally had her cornered, just as she had cornered me so many times to beat on me and ensure I feared her wrath if I ever exposed her secrets.

With only one class left, the door was blocked by the teacher. "My sister is here, I just know it," I said. "I saw her run down here, and this is the last class to check." Despite his attempt to turn me away and deny any knowledge of what I was rambling about, I ducked under his arm and entered the classroom, finding her washing her hands.

I still didn't understand what I walked into. I had so many questions, but I knew something was very, very wrong here. But what was I to say? All I saw was her washing her hands. I still had no hard proof or understanding of what was really going on.

As we concluded the lesson on abuse that week, I couldn't hold it together any longer. Exhaustion consumed me to the point where I felt there was barely any life left within me. My teacher escorted me from class straight to the guidance counselor, where I began to open up about the hell I had been enduring and what I had witnessed with my sister that I couldn't explain. They called my mom and connected us with a counselor at a mental health clinic. I was weary, as if I hadn't slept in the four years since that spring morning when she first put her hands on me.

I poured out what was left of my soul to that counselor, telling her every detail I knew, desperate for her to help me find the missing pieces to make it all make sense. That day, I didn't get any answers. But I did receive a look of disapproval, as I had just broken the biggest rule in our family: what happens in this family, stays in this family. I had exposed one of the biggest, darkest events that would ever hit our family.

To make it worse, my parents were convinced I was making it all up. Why would I keep something like that from them—and for so long? They couldn't understand how I could fear my own sister as deeply as I did. No way this teacher would be inappropriate in any way; he was so loved! I thought this would be my day of freedom, but it seemed as though that day would be delayed a bit longer.

As desperate as I was for help that day, I wasn't prepared to pay the toll it took on my family. I felt responsible, perhaps I had spoken too soon. The animosity between my sister and I grew exponentially as I was so close to exposing her in a way that would also provide proof. I kept a close watch, even closing in on her at home as I would see her coming from a field on the other side of our neighbor's house. Why on Earth would she be over there? The closer I came to finding solid answers, the more drastic measures my sister took.

It wasn't long after I confided everything I knew to the counselor that my sister's eyes were nearly as dark as coal. We got off the bus one day and all I heard was, "Run." I stumbled up the five steps to our side door, fumbling for my house key. Desperate for the bus to stay a little longer, I knew that as soon as it pulled away, my sister would be hot on my heels, as we say down here in North Cackalacky.

I got the door opened and beelined right through the kitchen into my bedroom, locking myself in. My sister began beating on my bedroom door, promising to kill me once she got her hands on me. I heard her go back into the kitchen, fumbling for a knife to pry the door open. I tried to push my desk in front of my bedroom door, but it wouldn't budge. All that was left to do was brace for impact. I prayed like never before, "God, just let it end quickly. Haven't I been through enough?"

My sister pried the door open and started kicking me . . . and that's all I remember.

> **God held me in His arms that day, and that was the first day He felt truly alive to me.**

While I was in the fetal position, I could see her kicking me, yet I couldn't feel anything but His protection enveloping me.

While it felt like an eternity, I am sure it was merely only seconds, at most minutes, before my mom walked in through the door early from work. She questioned what was going on and why in the world did my sister have a knife? I didn't hear anything as I was enamored with the fact that I was just held by my God.

It was that moment that He was no longer just God; rather, He became my Father. I had been embraced by my heavenly Father, and I didn't know if I should be going back to the mental health clinic or if I had just stepped into a whole other level of faith.

CHAPTER 3

Runaways

Our 1,200 square foot brick home was nestled on a decent lot. The front yard met the road fairly quickly, but not before the "great escape tunnel" that resided in our ditch. That ditch still gives me nightmares, and I am sure my dad can still feel the strain on his muscles when he thinks of it.

This ditch was so steep, great, and wide, that only he was allowed to maintain the overgrowth. There was a massive drain tunnel right in the middle of it that we'd joke could lead to China. At the very least, it led to the woods behind the pastor's house, which was across the street. It was so massive that we could walk through it while standing tall.

The road that separated us was not a busy road, but it was known for accidents. I am not sure if a month went by that we didn't hear the screeching of tires, and we would all cringe and brace for impact as though we were in the car ourselves.

Along the west end of our home ran a cotton field. I always thought it was so beautiful in full bloom. In the off season, I liked to go out into the field just to see how far I could hit a softball. The dirt was always so well maintained that my softballs would just bury themselves upon impact.

This field ran a long way, further than our eyes could see. Alongside the cotton field was the old train track. Sometime during our residency at that home, they turned it into a walking trail that expanded approximately seven miles. They called it the Rail Trail, and it connected the two neighboring towns. Yet, it was known by our family to cause the greatest disconnect.

I had yet to find answers to the chaos I was living in. I allowed the dust to settle and tried not to cause a lot of uproar. I knew that the little I had exposed was taking a toll on my parents, and not having those answers, I believe, made it worse for all of us. I was hot on my sister's trail; I could feel it. With deep conviction, I knew that all would be revealed by the end of my freshman year.

"SHE'S GONE AGAIN!" I heard my mom yell out to my dad with deep agony and wailing.

I rolled off my bed, flung open my bedroom door, and ran outside to find out what was going on. It wasn't the first time my sister ran away, certainly not the first time she had disappeared. This day was different. She'd been gone for hours rather than minutes. She did it without care for the hour of the day.

I don't believe she had the capacity to understand how deeply her actions cut into our family. It was only a matter of time before those cuts would divide us all.

Though our hearts were frantically beating, we looked around the neighborhood. We had to keep our composure and act as though there was no sheer panic and discord running deep within our family. Still, as the sun began to set, there was no sign of my sister. We had checked all the normal hideouts. Physically, emotionally, and spiritually weary, I believed we just could not continue fighting with my sister—for my sister. It was a new place of hopelessness none of us had ever experienced before.

That night, we carried on with life, compelling ourselves to gather around our family table and eat. There was an empty seat. No one spoke a word as we picked at our food, trying to recall conversations we had with my sister, hoping to uncover some clue as to where she could be. But my investigative mind turned on me, and I found myself in the hot seat, interrogating myself.

"Why do you care? She's gone, she can't torment you anymore! Just let her go and move on with life; this is your freedom!" I'd look up to see the anger on my dad's face and the anguish in my mother's eyes. I was desperate to relieve them of this pain. I took full responsibility for what was happening.

I excused myself from the dinner table and proceeded to clean the kitchen. She should have been there with me. It was my job to put away the leftovers and take out the scraps, while my sister started washing the dishes, and then I would help finish up by rinsing them. Tonight was different. She was gone. My parents were paralyzed with emotion at the dinner table.

Gathering the scraps, I headed outside to toss them on the edge of that cotton field as per the routine. As I looked out across the field, my spirit told me, "she's here." Intently, I scanned the field as I walked a few rows in. Though the field was not in bloom, the cane still remained waist-high. I stood there, surrounded by silence, straining my ears to hear something. Moments passed, and I ignored my spirit's previous accusations that my 16-year-old sister was lying low in the soil. Turning, I started walking back toward my house, while I looked across the yard and saw our childhood play out before me. I lost hope that I would ever see her again; despite the hell she put me through, I still wanted the best for her.

I heard a call out. Wondering if I was imagining it, I jumped back into the field, hurdling over the cane stalks, yelling out her name. Rustling reached my ears—was it my sister, or another stray cat coming for the scraps I had just thrown out?

My pleas echoed into our home as my parents came running out. Continuing to yell, I was nearly thirty rows deep into the field, halfway to the Rail Trail at this point.

Pushing myself past exhaustion, I sprinted down the rows, pausing moments in between, fervently seeking to grab ahold of another call out or to actually see her. If I could just bring her home tonight, perhaps it would relieve my parents enough to find a glimpse of hope to find help for my sister—none of us could give it to her.

That night, my dad pulled me out of the field. I was furious with him. With every fiber of my being, I knew she was in there, and I was so close. I just needed more time.

Three days passed, and still, no sight or word from my sister. We didn't have cell phones, so the chances of her calling were slim to none. Every day that passed, our hearts prepared for the worst.

While I thought I was so close to finding answers to explain the last five years of hell I endured, my mind raced with a fresh new set of questions desperate for answers.

I'll never forget the day I saw the squad car pull into our driveway. I knew that regardless of the "what happens in this house stays in this house" rule, there would be nothing our family could do to contain it all today.

I watched as the officer opened the back passenger door and I saw my sister step out. I ran past my parents, still paralyzed in their emotions, and embraced my sister. I knew that what the officer was saying was not my business, but I took advantage of my parents' paraplegic state and hoped for answers to my questions.

"She hitchhiked across the state, she was found in Myrtle Beach," the officer explained. I locked eyes on my sister as if I could prevent her from running again if I just fixed my eyes on her. While we were left perplexed and angry at the chaos she had caused in our lives, she smiled.

Why was she smiling? I was frustrated not having any answers to my questions, so I just blurted it out. "WHY ARE YOU SMIL-ING?! This isn't funny. We were all so worried, we scoured the neighborhood for you. I even searched the field for you."

"I know," she said with a smirk that just disgusted me. It's as though my parents and the officer faded away. I didn't see the neighbors gathering or hear anything but my sister's voice.

"You were so close to finding me, I was just three more rows over. I can't believe you didn't find me." She started to laugh with the smirk still on her face.

I was sickened and so angry. This was all a joke to her; she had no remorse for anything. I stepped back and began to head toward the front door of our home. I had had enough. I was done searching for my answers, I was done chasing her down, protecting her. I was simply . . . done.

She proceeded to tell my parents, with the officer still there, "She was right about everything." She then exposed all the details of one of the biggest scandals that had hit our little town at that time.

Five years. For five years, I desperately searched for answers, and I was finally finding out just how close I was when I found her washing her hands in the far building of our school. I was always so close, within reach even of finding her, exposing the alternate life she had created for herself.

My sister was transported to Dorothea Dix Hospital that day. We believed she was on her way to get help and treatment, to find answers deeper than I ever thought to search before. We met them at the hospital, and while we left moments after them, we arrived first. I still remember the smell walking in the hospital that day and hearing the occasional outburst of screams and obscene yelling from patients. I wasn't sure this was where my sister belonged, but I trusted my parents were acting with the best of intentions for my sister and our family. The officer arrived with my sister, and they began the intake paperwork. Honestly, everything was a bit of a blur after that.

It was later discovered that my sister shared with a counselor about her ride to Dorothea Dix Hospital. Yet, another scandal. While my parents were told that they were running behind because they stopped for gas, it seems they left out a few details.

The officer stopped and had a sexual interaction with my sister before making it to the hospital. Given the circumstances of the situation we were all still trying to digest, the media was on high alert. My sister's story was now circulating in media outlets and the streets of our small town. Complete with a multitude of ad libs from all around, my family was under a spotlight we never wanted and tried effortlessly to avoid at all costs.

The very thing that started this whole mess long ago with teachers was now happening with an officer of the law. As though what we had heard thus far wasn't sickening enough, tainting all trust with authority of any sorts, this just pushed my family over a meta-phoric edge—I was not convinced we would ever recover.

While her name was never mentioned because she was a minor, it seemed everyone knew exactly who was involved. It was as if everyone had the answers to the questions I spent years searching for long before our family did. I remember my parents trying to prepare me for what life may look like finishing out my years at my current high school. But I had friends and I was never a big fan of change. I wanted to stay.

Even though everything else was turned upside down in my life, I felt I could control this and leaned on my friends to get me through. I quickly found out exactly who my true friends were. The news was spreading like wildfire and it was spiraling out of control. Everyone wanted to know the inside scoop, and God showed me through my season what a true friend is.

There were only two that remained true. They never asked for details. In fact, the only conversation they had about it was, "If you want to talk about it, we're here to listen; otherwise, I'll see you at break in our usual spot." They were a solid foundation for me and were intentional about inserting normalcy in my life. That is the reason why we are still friends to this day, regardless of the distance between us.

Unfortunately, the majority saw an opportunity to wreak havoc on my life. Sex offers by peers, comments about meeting a guy in the bathroom or down by the football field, as was reported to have happened with my sister, became a daily occurrence. Being groped in the classroom while teachers were distracted, or cornered in a hallway, was a normal occurrence for me. Broken promises from the principal that these peers would face suspension only deepened the humiliation I was feeling.

Only one out of the four teachers that I knew were directly involved in an inappropriate relationship with my sister was prosecuted. That doesn't include the teachers that knew what was happening and helped cover it up. Seeing them as I walked the halls of my high school just sickened me. They were wrong regardless if they had sexual interactions with her, gave her jewelry, or if they simply accepted her phone call. They took advantage of her and indirectly made my life a living hell for years.

It is truly fascinating to me how many of us go through life and never count the costs of our actions.

> **Whether a positive or negative impact, everything we do has a ripple effect to those in our family and community.**

It was my senior year before the dust settled after two years of just having to walk the halls with people I truly felt should be in jail for their actions with my sister, but also dealing with my peers. My teachers supported me, protected me, and yet also allowed space for me to grow and process the magnitude of the situation.

They echoed over me that I had to choose how the rest of my life would play out. My grades suffered, and despite my situation, they did not pity me. Rather, they pushed me. Pushed me toward greatness. Pushed me to find who I was again because we all knew it had been tarnished and warped in the cast of my sister's shadow.

I graduated high school in 2005 and, to my great surprise, my role model tapped me on the shoulder and said, "You did it, today you graduate with honors." I have no idea how I pulled that one off, but I knew I worked hard to fight back and finish stronger than I started.

My grandmother passed away before my graduation that year, unexpectedly to me, yet it seemed expected to my family. She was my best friend; we had plans for our future. I was going to move in with her after high school. We would travel together (she did not drive) and find all the best places to play bingo along the way. I felt like my future was ripped from me as soon as I had just started finding hope again.

Life at home was hard. It wasn't long before I was the only one left sitting at the dinner table, with Jerry Springer piercing the silence. I never understood why they always watched that show; my God, we were living out our own episode. I cried in silence many nights at that table, grieving what used to be, praying that my parents would find the strength to live again.

After graduation, I decided to move out that summer in an attempt to piece my life back together. I was working as a waitress at a franchise restaurant and had received two scholarships for computer science, due to start in the fall. It felt like the right next step for me. I sat my parents down in the living room and shared my plans with them. I was only moving across town, with a teacher nonetheless. She was new to the area and was someone I felt safe with.

Having shared the news with my parents, I went out with friends to celebrate all we had accomplished and made our plans for all that was to come. While I listened to them, I found myself becoming angry as I realized my plans were not MY dream. I wanted to teach PE and coach softball and basketball. So why in the world was I about to start college for computer science? Why couldn't I just move in with my grandmother and fulfill our dreams together as planned? Why was no one but me surprised at her passing?

I spiraled . . . HARD! I didn't know what I would do, but I knew I was ready to go home.

As I pulled into the driveway, I noticed my belongings lined up along the sidewalk where my dad's blue Chevy Silverado was parked. It was a newer model now, a darker shade of blue than before. I just looked at my things, feeling a sense of displacement, and glanced back at the basketball court. Reliving my life here, I desperately clung to any good memories that I could, looking across the yard where my dad became my catcher as I dreamed of being the next great pitcher for our small town.

I caught the gaze of both of my dogs, and even they knew something just wasn't right. Without a word, I packed my belongings into my car and drove away. Away from so much hurt and pain. Away from the silence that deafened us. Somewhere between the sobbing and anger, my mindset shifted from moving out and starting my life like a typical college kid . . . to running away.

I ran with an intensity that would surely end with a catastrophic collision.

CHAPTER 4

My Search for Family

I used all the emotion I could muster, the adrenaline, to get moved into the house off Highway 95. Thankfully, my roommate had a bed and dresser for me as I couldn't bring mine with me. I took a deep breath and just let the tears fall where they may. A sense of relief washed over me as the terrible season was finally over. I was overwhelmed to be starting college . . . angry and regretful that I did not choose to follow my dream . . . perplexed that my parents really just left all of my belongings packed in the driveway. In a way, I felt betrayed. This isn't how I thought my next season would start. I thought there would be more celebration and support. I thought I'd be surrounded by family regardless where I lived.

I was desperate to have a family, one that would remind me of what used to be before the great scandal and reminded me of who I was created to be—the real me. So I took to the internet, searching for a family to call my own in a Christian chat room. It was my first time exploring chat rooms, but I felt it would be safe since it was classified as Christian. I did classes throughout the day and worked whenever I could pick up shifts, which was nearly every day at a certain point. That left late nights and wee hours of the morning for Worthy Chat—the Christian chat room I chose.

My first time logging in, I was skeptical and broken, and I thought I had nothing to lose. I wouldn't be as vulnerable since, more than likely, I'd never see these people in person. I would be safe. The first name I saw as I entered the chat was Mama LeeLee, and there was an instant connection. Perhaps it was the name, but fast forwarding eighteen years to today, I know without a doubt she was strategically placed in my life by God. I was introduced to the regulars, moderators, and welcomed in with open arms. Life was going well, and I felt like I was going to be okay, eventually.

I kept myself busy with school, work, even helping out at church on Wednesday nights with none other than Ms. Lee, who by that time had become Momma Donna. While I started making good friends in Worthy Chat, they couldn't keep my feelings compressed. It was in the late nights that my feelings would come in like an unmerciful flood. The grief of my grandmother was not going away, and I had no idea what to do with it. She was the first great loss in my life, and I was left to figure out how to process it on my own.

We tend to become a product of our environment. While I had no desire to see another episode of Jerry Springer, there wasn't a day I could remember my parents not having a beer in their hands. I couldn't stand the smell of beer long enough to even take a sip. I was eighteen years old and determined to find something to numb the pain. My roommate had daiquiris in the fridge, so that's where I started. Three drinks later, I felt this could be my hope to stifle my pain and grief. My roommate wasn't very happy that I helped myself to her drinks. While I was still underage, she offered to purchase alcohol for me. And that's all I needed—that's where my experimenting began and the worst spiral I ever experienced.

I was still keeping up with my classes and work. My relationship with Mama LeeLee was growing stronger every day. We Skyped every day as soon as I got home. There were a few years I even purchased calling cards so I could call her regardless of where I was. I was running so hard nonstop, I started drinking Red Bulls and experimenting with speed to keep my momentum. I never wanted to end my day without having my time with Mama LeeLee. I felt like I could tell her anything without condemnation. I began to tell her the story I share with you here.

It wasn't a coincidence that the echoes of my former teachers would ring through just as Mama LeeLee did as well, adamant to remind me that I was created with purpose and my choices now would dictate where my life would lead. You'd think that having so many showing up in life, echoing the same words, would have reminded me of when my Father held me in my bedroom years prior. You'd think that would have jolted me enough to lean into my Father's arms and realize He is my family, He is my everything.

Yet, I found myself having my roommate buy me another case of Smirnoff every other day. While I could sense her concern, she continued to enable my addiction. It felt easier to drown my mountain of emotions in alcohol than to battle the voices in my head telling me I was unworthy of love: too broken to be fixed, too hurt to ever trust again. I started missing classes and showing up late for work. It was a slow fade.

That's how it happens. That's how we are deceived, thinking we have everything under control because it happens slowly. Going through it, you don't realize the spiritual world doesn't work the same on this side of Heaven. While your slow fade is happening on this side, our spirit takes the downfall at twice the speed in the heavenly realm. Every bottle I drank pushed me further away from God. I struggled to even call him Father for the longest time.

It was in that house off Highway 95 that I entered into a spiritual realm I never knew I asked to be in. Playing around with sin will open doors that'll leave you begging God for mercy, and it will be only His mercy that will be able to close them. To be honest, telling this part of my story still terrifies me. It is still so tangible and vivid as though it is happening all over again. I feel the fear rising inside this very moment. I feel that if I speak of the things they did to me and the power the shadowy, demonic spirits had over me, it will empower them in my life today.

Just say the name of Jesus . . .

Thankfully, my God is bigger, and I will not be silenced.

My hope is that my story will empower you to fight the darkness in your own life.

It started with shadows outside.

The old brick home was plotted next to a field. Our landlords lived right in front of us, a mere thirty yards away. Was this ironic? I suppose so. It was often that we'd see the shadows out in the yard. I used to try and rationalize what I was experiencing for the longest time. I'd be in the kitchen making another bowl of ramen and grabbing another Smirnoff from the fridge, and I'd catch a glimpse of them through the dining room window covered with thin curtains. It wasn't long at all before those shadows started appearing in my house. They were no longer shielded by the curtains.

I know what you're thinking . . . I was drunk, hallucinating, probably tripping on speed. No, I had already flushed what speed I had left and was long past that.

I have searched for years for the words to express the reality that I was experiencing. I suppose you'll have to take my word as true, and I hope you do, in case you find yourself in an epic battle for your soul. With all of the abuse I endured throughout my life, I still to this day have never been more tormented than my final months in that house off Highway 95.

I don't actually have much recollection of the first time I realized I was dealing with something more than just mere shadows. I remember coming home and going directly to my desk that was in the corner of the living room. I logged into "Worthy Chat," and that's it. While I didn't see any shadows that day, there was a sense of darkness surrounding me. I walked away from my computer and started my day as normal. It was the anger on my roommate's face that made me question things. Later that day, we talked. It was safer that we did, as we could both sense the weight of emotion in the room that morning.

"Why didn't you respond to me?" she retorted. I had no idea what she was talking about. I had gone to see her in her classroom at the school after my own classes that day. It's when I noticed the date on her whiteboard, and it was then that I knew something was terribly wrong. There was a whole day completely unaccounted for. I fought to remember anything that had happened. All I could get was walking through the house and to my computer in the living room. That was it. I don't know who I spoke to or what I may have done. My roommate caught on pretty quickly that I had experienced something I truly would not be able to recollect, perhaps ever. I asked her if she had seen the shadows; it was then we knew we had opened doors to hell that needed to be sealed shut.

Did we actually open them? While I am not totally convinced I opened them, I know I was pushing God as far away as possible. While I may not have initially opened the doors of darkness in the house, I know I was living a life of sin.

> **I know the separation I created between myself and God left me vulnerable to experiences I would have otherwise been protected from.**

My roommate and I shared the feeling of being trapped in that house before. We both experienced something sitting on our chests in bed, making us unable to move or call out for help. Feeling as crazy as I did, she confided in me, and we struggled to understand what we were dealing with. How do you share such experiences with others? We knew we sounded insane, but it was the harsh reality we found ourselves subjected to. On many nights when these experiences occurred, I would find myself fleeing the house and speeding off in my car as soon as I was "released" from the hold these spirits had on me. I'd drive across town to Mrs. Ferg's house, a kind woman from our church. She always left a blanket and pillow on the couch for me and the back door unlocked, providing a safe place for me to escape, which I did many nights throughout that year.

It was Mama LeeLee who first called out my drinking. Out of respect, I never drank in front of her, fearing she would see my brokenness, especially due to my own choices. Out of nowhere, she asked, "Baby Girl, why have you started drinking?" I tried to deny it, but it was her tone and posture. It felt as if my spirit knew my Father wasn't giving up on me; He was chasing me down, this time using a lady all the way in the United Kingdom. I wish I could say that was when I decided to get sober.

December 2, 2005, I woke up feeling terrible. I kept having sharp pains in my stomach and felt feverish. Surviving on alcohol, ramen, and Red Bull, I wondered why I wasn't feeling well. I called my boss and let him know I was unwell.

Remember that slow fade I told you about? Well, my boss had enough of it. I went from being a trainer and working toward management to now being told that if I don't come in, I would be fired. I had no choice; I had to go in. I couldn't lose my job on top of everything else I already felt I had lost in the last five years. I put on my uniform, climbed into my little red Chevy Cavalier, and made my way down the abandoned country back roads. It was the first time I remember talking to God in a long time.

I begged for mercy and contemplated forfeiting my job and making my way to the hospital. It seemed the further I got down the road, the pain intensified. Another sharp stab to my abdomen and everything went dark. I remember my car going up on its nose and then I saw . . . Tyeisha? The daughter of Momma Donna, the one I called sister, the one that was taken too soon in a car accident the year prior. She spoke to me so clearly and said, "Just look at me, you're going to be okay, sis." I couldn't speak, my eyes fixed on Ty and wanting to ask so many questions, but I had apparently lost the ability to speak. Was I dreaming?

As soon as Ty left, I was fully aware of where I was, held in by my seatbelt, and I realized my car had landed on the passenger side. I was stuck in my seatbelt, scared of what would happen if I unfastened it. Then, a man appeared on top of my car and said, "You're okay, just unfasten it and grab my hand." I remember the smell of dirt and immediately flashed back to the old cotton field from my childhood home; had I somehow landed there? I unfastened my seatbelt and dropped to the passenger side of the car. I looked up and saw this stranger reaching down through my driver window to take hold of my hand. I didn't have any choice but to trust him, but there was something in his eyes that filled me with peace. I took hold of his hand; he pulled me up so effortlessly. I never touched my car. I was pulled straight up and placed in the field where my car had landed.

Then, he was gone. He never gave a name; there was no one around, no vehicles even on this back road. I called out several times, "Hello! Sir? Thank you?" My car was totaled . . . I started walking through the field and made eye contact with the older lady that lived across the street. It was as though she was expecting me. A small, round, cast iron table sat in her front yard with two plastic chairs. She was still bringing out the glass of water before I made it across the street. Her smile welcomed me and she said, "Come, sit, have some water, call your mother."

Despite the questions racing through my mind, I simply did as she directed. I called my mother and all I could say was "I'm okay, but I've been in an accident." As soon as I sat down, the road was blocked with traffic. I'd never seen so many cars on this road before in my life. Fire and rescue had arrived; three squad cars were on site as well. I felt as though I was watching a movie play out in front of me and I was the main character. I heard the rescue team yell out, "There's no one in the car; it's really bad. This will be a recovery. We need to find the body."

I couldn't move. I couldn't even speak. I even tried small talk with the elderly lady sitting with me. I felt like everything was happening in slow motion. Whatever "this" was, was over as I heard my mother's voice pleading, "Where's my daughter?"

I thanked the lady and went to meet my mother on the road. It had been a while since I felt her embrace.

"Are you okay? We should take you to the hospital," she said.

"No, no, I am ok," I said.

Needless to say, I didn't make it to work that day after all, but I did update them and I was given a grace card.

I went home and replayed the events over and over again. Was it all a dream? Where did that man go? Who was he?

> **I knew it was another encounter with my Father I would not soon forget.**

My car accident really shook me to my core. I found myself consumed with replaying the reel of that day over and over again. Why would God spare me, yet again?

I attempted to start fighting for my sobriety. I was desperate to find out why my life was worth saving. What did my Father see in me, and why couldn't I see it for myself? It wasn't easy, and I found myself unable to stop cold turkey, but I made an honest attempt to limit my consumption more every day until it was no more.

I was on the right track.

I started sharing my story with others in Worthy Chat and became pretty close with a married couple that happened to be moderators. They had a five-year-old son, that very quickly felt like a little brother to me. They were from Tennessee and starting a ministry with family friends.

I was three months shy from turning nineteen and intently focused on finding purpose for my life.

Between my obsession with finding a family that would love me for who I was and feeling indebted to God, it didn't take a whole lot to convince me to move to Tennessee and help build this ministry. There was no monetary promise but there was a glimpse of hope for my future. I knew joining this ministry would also connect me with sobriety that I was desperately searching for. It would hold me accountable and keep me focused on something bigger than myself.

I packed my belongings and called a friend for a ride since my car had been totaled in the accident. Although I was swirling in a flood of emotions toward my parents, unable to define what it was I was feeling toward them, I found it only respectful to share my plans with them.

I informed the college I was attending that I was dropping out. I don't think they were too shocked, considering I was kicking robots across the classroom out of rage for not getting them to operate correctly and the inability to understand my Chinese math professor beyond "TA-DA" after he solved a math problem.

Perhaps the hardest part was giving my two weeks' notice with my employer. I was working exactly where my grandmother always wanted me to, so she could enjoy discounts on her chili cheese fries. Leaving would also mean leaving a piece of her behind.

It was time to leave this small town, where the streets were etched with my past, construed by gossip, and the shadow of my sister. It was time to write my own story.

CHAPTER 5

Tennessee

It was February 18. We drove through the night to make it to Knoxville, Tennessee just in time for Matt's sixth birthday. Early that morning, before pulling into the driveway of what was now home, we stopped at Food Lion. He specified he wanted an ice cream cake. Not just any ice cream cake, an M&M ice cream cake! Now, I don't know if this boy saw this in the store before and had his heart set on it for months leading up to his special day, but don't you know I walked right in and found exactly that! That's how God works! He's just that good at focusing on the details that make us smile a little bigger than before.

Matt was the son of two Worthy Chat moderators who quickly became "mom and dad" to me. They had promised me a safe haven, agreeing that God didn't accidentally place me in theater for six years for no reason; rather, He wanted to use it for His glory. Their ministry would be the place it would all unfold. But it was Matt who truly had my whole heart. There was just something about him that resonated with me.

While discussing details of my arrival the month prior, I was asked, "What color did I want my room?" After everything I had been through and my natural gift of sarcasm, I responded, "I don't care, paint it polka dots for all I care!" After indulging in his ice cream cake for breakfast, Matt was so excited to show me my room. It was the last bedroom on the right. I closed my eyes; "mom" placed her hands over them, more excited than me for the grand reveal at this point.

"1 . . . 2 . . . 3 . . . OPEN!" The house erupted with laughter. I couldn't remember the last time I laughed as genuinely and as hard until that day. Yep, there were polka dots alright! All sorts of sizes, different colors, some left unpainted as there just wasn't enough time before my arrival.

Everything was perfect for the first few weeks. I met the pastor of this new ministry; we discussed creating a worship team and what that would look like. His daughter and I bonded fairly quickly with our shared passion for worship. There were seven of us kids between the two families. I was the oldest and very protective of this new family of mine.

We lived in this pretty cool neighborhood; it was nice and well kept. At the end of the road, nearly a mile from our house, was the school Matt attended. I'd never seen a school in a neighborhood like this before. I enjoyed running. It helped me process my emotions, so I would run to the school every day to pick up Matt. We'd talk about his day, and he'd try his best to outrun me. This kid, man I loved him so much . . . still do.

I began to catch a glimpse into a secret he was hiding: he was being bullied pretty bad. It wasn't just name-calling; they would take his shoes off and throw them up in the trees, knock him down, and kick him around. One day, I witnessed it, and it set a trigger off in me. I sprinted harder than ever before to make it to my lil guy, yelling for them to leave him alone. I picked him up off the ground and just hugged him the way my Father held me in my bedroom years prior.

> **I knew God was trying to get me to see the parallel of how He chases after me.**

His love for me was so deep. Matt, too.

Home life began to shift and change. I suddenly found myself with a schedule and a list of chores. My whole day was planned—everything from when to read my Bible, when to pray, how long to pray, and when I could eat. Most of my chores included caring for their son. While I loved him, what was being asked of me was the role of a parent, and I was not that. While I questioned this and wondered what was happening, I was desperate to just be accepted and loved, so I complied.

When we didn't, we were punished. Eighteen years old and having a paddle taken to my backside or grounded to my room. Rock punishment was one of the more grueling ones. We would be made to choose two landscape stones and hold them out to our sides. If our arms dropped, we had to start over, and we were swatted with a paddle. The humiliation, shame, and regret started to reside in me again.

I came here to do God's will—to build a ministry. While I may not have all the instructions to what it takes to build a ministry, I knew this was not what it was meant to look like. My desperation for acceptance left me submitting to this way of life for a while before I started fighting back. The more I tried to correct the family I was living with and explain this wasn't the way, the more I was punished into silence.

Matt also endured a lot. I had never seen a child taught how to read or spell by paddling them for every mistake. I was experiencing a new anger that scared even me. I was ready to physically fight back at all costs. This wasn't anger, this was a holy rage unleashing inside of me.

Many times, I would jump in front of Matt to protect him from their blows. It wasn't right. His stepdad was the worst. I remember we were told to pack our stuff, we were moving to Crossville. Apparently, that's where God needed us the most, as there was a porn shop or liquor store on every street corner.

Matt broke down. At just six years old, he was exhausted from the life he was enduring. Poor guy still could not begin to comprehend what was going on and how this was love. I came to his room and gave him space to feel everything, to vent it all out to me. I stood in the doorway and watched him fall to the floor in his closet, surrounded by his toys and boxes of clothes, being told he couldn't take it all by his parents.

I worked to console him, offering to stash his toys in my boxes. If it meant this boy would have some peace, I would have left all of my stuff behind in that house. I found myself on the floor of his closet, just holding him, letting the tears fall where they may. Then, his stepdad stormed through the door with rage in his eyes and a belt in his hand, convinced that beating this boy would bring about his silence.

I stood between them and pushed his stepdad back to the doorway. "Just leave him alone," I said. "Beat me if you must, but don't touch him again." I don't think this burly, middle-aged man was afraid of me. I had to believe that God stepped into that room with me and Matt that day, and it was His presence that sent him away without another word.

I know what you're thinking: what about the ministry? Was it all a scam? Well, it wasn't a scam. We still led worship, mime, and interpretive dancing on Sunday mornings and Wednesday nights. Just every day in between, behind the closed doors, left me regretting my decision to move to Tennessee.

The five kids belonging to the pastor were living the same hell as me and Matt. It just seemed there were more screams of mercy than laughter and joy that started my life in Tennessee. We stood together, protecting each other as much as we could.

What broke me more than anything is, I chose to move here, and if I could ever get the courage to leave, I could escape. But the rest of them, this is their natural born family. There weren't as many choices for them. The pastor's family was a blended family; before I parted ways, three of them went to live with their other parent. Two of them remained with the pastor and his wife.

As for me and Matt, if I close my eyes and go back to Crossville in my mind, I can still feel his arms locked around my waist. I can still hear his pleas for me to take him with me. I still feel the guilt of leaving him behind. I should have done more; I should have fought for him, called CPS, something, anything. I could not rise above my cowardice. I too was exhausted from the battle we had been fighting.

I reunited with Matt a few years ago through Facebook. While it was difficult to hear of the passing of his mom, stepdad, and biological dad, and all the battles he had to fight on his own, he allowed me the opportunity to apologize. Although he said it wasn't needed, he understood. It was a weight lifted. While Matt said he was back on the straight and narrow with life, I know what addiction looks like and the infamous lines commonly used.

My heart breaks to see his struggle, but I can't be an enabler, and that is a hard reality to have to come to grips with—especially when you love someone so deeply. I will always love him as my brother, and my prayers will always cover him. I know God will continue to chase him down until he accepts everything God created him to be. He will do the same for YOU too.

> **At some point, each of us is the "one" that our Father leaves the ninety-nine for.**

I moved in with a friend from work to escape Crossville, but I remained in Tennessee for a while longer, working at the local Cracker Barrel just trying to survive. I gave up hope on a bright future for myself. Unfortunately, I fell back into my alcoholism, drinking every night, and there was no preference at this point. I just wanted to drown my guilt of leaving Matt behind in anything I could get my hands on, to numb the pain—my only agenda for each new day.

I met a guy, and we started dating. He was kind and respectful, a good ol' country boy. He worked during the day, and I took a break from the work life and found my way back to Worthy Chat. I was thrilled to reconnect with Mama LeeLee. While we had some contact during my time in Crossville, I was forbidden to speak to her. I caught her up on what really went on in that ministry, and we vowed to never speak of it again.

While Mama LeeLee was excited to reconnect, we didn't talk as much as we used to, which we both felt was a healthier balance. She certainly wasn't fond of me moving in with my boyfriend, but what could she do but send a warning?

I moved in with him and two of his other friends. That house was so unique. It sat up on a hill, and going anywhere in the winter was a challenge with the ice and snow. The first part was pretty traditional, other than the spiral staircase in the living room that led to a hexagon-shaped foyer and two smaller rooms. Another three steps up from that foyer was a platform. Imagine the top of a lighthouse; this is what it reminded me of. This was the newer side of the home, while the older portion of the home was actually round. We called it the round house, as if it had its own identity.

The second floor had three bedrooms and a bathroom, and there was a large open area on the first floor. Unfortunately, the only memories I really hold of this house are drowning in hard liquor. I was consuming anything that would numb the pain and silence what my heart knew were lies, but I couldn't bring myself to receive the truth God was still trying so fervently to remind me of.

One night, I drank myself to a slumber, passing out in one of the bedrooms in the round house, which only had a mattress on the floor and a dresser in the corner. When I opened my eyes, I saw five guys standing around my mattress, just watching me and having conversations, but I could not understand any of it. I yelled at myself from within, "GET UP, GET OUT, DO SOMETHING!" I don't know if it was the fear of what they could have been discussing or my heavy breathing of panic in the darkened room that had me rolling off the mattress and running, knelt over to the bathroom, and violently vomiting, missing the toilet and now covered in my own spew.

> **I can't rule out the possibility that even God Himself would move me to such a violent sickness to save me from myself.**

I cleaned myself up the best I could with a pounding headache, feeling my stomach doing contortions. Then, I crawled into the first bedroom where my boyfriend was also in a drunken slumber and fell back to sleep. The next day, we made plans to move to a vacant family property that was sitting on his grandfather's farm.

It was an old farmhouse, with the front door sticking at times and creaking when opened. As soon as we entered the front door, there was an old wood-burning stove in the small living room. Off to the right of the living room, there was a large bedroom with its own entrance to the outside world. This would be my bedroom, while my boyfriend slept in the bedroom off of the kitchen.

Yes, at nineteen years old, I was still a virgin. I had made the same vow many did in the 1990s and received a purity ring at summer camp. Despite all the mistakes I had made, at least I could hold true to that. The house had a stagnant smell throughout, but it would be ours, and we vowed to start fresh and sober up.

Behind the house was a large oak tree where I loved to sit and write in my journal. This tree was rooted next to a cow-filled pasture, which I initially thought was cool to have as neighbors. However, that glory disappeared quickly with the late-night wake-up calls and disturbing mating sounds that rang through the night. It's not a sound you will soon forget, let's just say that.

We did get to witness the birth of a calf and had to help nurse it to health, all the while praying we wouldn't be charged by its mom. Farm life, it's not for the faint of heart!

It seemed the more I wrote and reflected on my life and how abuse just seemed to follow me, the more angry I became with God. I cursed Him in that cow pasture without a fear in me. I am not sure if I can call my actions bold or stupid. I do feel God could have an appreciation that I was finally being 100 percent vulnerable and real with Him. While He knows everything about me, there's a freedom that comes with actually expressing every thought, every emotion.

> **If we can't be honest about what we're feeling, we can never begin to process and heal.**

God can handle your anger, grief, frustration . . . ALL of it. His arms are broad and wide; let Him have it.

I yelled, cussed, shook my fist at the heavens, and demanded answers for my life.

"Move." That's all I got, and I questioned if I was hearing the cows moo or if God was actually speaking and telling me to move.

We can find ourselves stuck in a victim mindset while living dark lives—whether by consequences of our own choices or simply by crossing paths with others who made poor decisions that affect us too. We own it so much deeper than we desire to claim hope, truth, and freedom. We grow weary from the fight and accept a fate that was never ours to claim.

> **God says, "Seek Me and you will find Me." When was the last time you played hide and seek without actually moving to go seek those that were hiding? If we are truly seeking God, and ultimately that's what I was asking for in that cow pasture, we have to move. Move past the hurt, pain, neglect, brokenness, and heartache. Catch His garment flowing from behind a door and follow it until you are standing with Him face to face.**

I couldn't just move out; I had nowhere to go. So, I did what I could. I took the next step and started searching for a job. I also broke up with my boyfriend, promising him I was actively looking for a job and would be out in three months.

It was right in the heart of winter, and moving was the last thing I wanted to do. But I contemplated it deeply and everything it could mean. I shared this with my friends and family in Worthy Chat, but most importantly, Mama LeeLee. She lit up with joy and hope. She had heard my story inside and out, seen me make some terrible decisions out of my pain, and now I was back to listening to my Father and I was remaining sober.

As expected, my ex-boyfriend (now) did not share the same enthusiasm with my new search for something deeper and wholesome. He went to work daily at a local factory assembling car parts on the midnight shift, and I stayed home searching for any work I could that would provide a substantial amount to make my move.

With his own brokenness consuming him and our plans dissembling as quickly as we had put them together, he closed the damper on the wood-burning stove so that the smoke had no way to escape.

I woke up with my lungs filling with smoke, my eyes burning. I rolled out of bed and ran out to the living room, desperately trying to open the old window but was only able to open it slightly—not near enough to bring any relief. I escaped outside and called 911 as I saw his grandfather running across the yard to come help. While there is no proof my ex did this intentionally, it was strongly suspected, as he knew very well how to operate the ins and outs of everything on the farm.

I felt I needed to make a move quickly, so I attempted a job at the factory to make transportation easier, as I still did not have a vehicle. I lasted approximately four hours, and those four hours were spent in tears as I developed blisters within thirty minutes. It is one of the few things I do remember quitting cold turkey in life. Much respect to factory workers!

The next week I was hired at Walmart and due to start orientation immediately. It wasn't what I wanted, but I was excited to be making a move in the right direction. My first night went great, and I was optimistic about getting my life back in order, becoming independent, and allowing God to work a ministry in me.

I was so excited to get home and share my hope with Mama LeeLee. I scooted into his old red Chevy S10 and started dreaming of what my future would look like and reiterated my promise that I would be out of his home soon. I was thankful for this grace period to get things lined up and was intentional to make sure he knew it.

That night took an abrupt turn of fate. I began to question if either of us would make it home as he began to swerve through the streets. He didn't say much as I pleaded with him to please just get us home safe, and I would find somewhere to go tonight and be out of his way. Thankfully, we did make it safely.

As I walked through the front door I saw my things thrown everywhere, the house was a complete disarray with my belongings. I regained my focus and started to clean it up, begging God to give me the next steps to make a move that night. He went into his room, and I noticed two bullets sitting on the wooden side table just as he was coming out of his bedroom, now standing in the doorway of the kitchen and living room.

We both made a lunge for the bullets, but he won that fight. He informed me that one was for me and one for himself, and he would be back to settle this once and for all.

I panicked. While I found myself yet in another dire situation, I wasn't angry with God this time—rather angry with myself. I called one of the moderators from Worthy Chat, Mike, on my phone and told him what was going on. Mike had been a part of Worthy Chat for years and held great authority there. He seemed to always be online and heard much of my story just as Mama LeeLee did.

I was terrified to call the cops, feeling they couldn't be trusted. But I was out of options. We were in the middle of nowhere, it was the dead of night, and if I didn't make a move soon, I would be dead within the hour. He convinced me to call the police for help, and he would arrange further details to get me away from Tennessee.

I called the police and prayed they'd make it back before my ex did. I saw his headlights pull into the old gravel drive but still could not hear sirens. I closed my eyes and prayed that God would forgive me and cleanse my heart of all the anger, unforgiveness, bitterness and judgment that I had not yet had a chance to work through.

"LINCOLN!!" I heard someone call out. I peeked through my eyes and there he stood, towering over me as I was knelt on the floor bracing for the impact. The cops made it in the nick of time. They talked him down, and let me gather my stuff while they spoke with him outside.

I left the house with as many belongings as I could carry, and was placed in the back of the squad car. It became apparent through bits and pieces of the interaction with the police that the responding officer was also Lincoln's best friend. Knowing this detail, everything could have ended much worse. I watched my ex go back into the house and turn off the porch light.

WHAT. JUST. HAPPENED? Of course, my mind began playing tapes from my past involving the police, and I was just sickened and so confused. Why am I the one being taken away like a criminal? I sat at the police station until about four o'clock in the morning before being transported to a women's shelter. I was told to stay quiet as families were sleeping. They'd do my intake in the morning. Go to bed.

I went to my room, locked my door and cried myself to sleep, wondering what tomorrow would hold for me.

CHAPTER 6

Captured

The next morning, I walked into the office of the women's shelter to meet with the director. "Let me just start with saying that I don't belong here. I am not staying. Don't waste your time with paperwork," I said adamantly. Over and over again, I repeated those words, knowing good and well I was not just trying to convince this director that sat before me. I too needed to be convinced—this was not my destiny.

I now wonder if perhaps that was exactly where God wanted me, and yet, my pride failed me. Perhaps that would have brought this nightmare to an end, and I'd learn to dream again.

I received a call from Mike while still in the office with the director. He informed me that he had purchased my Greyhound ticket to Minnesota. His advice was clear: get far away, let the dust of everything settle, and then I could return to North Carolina for a fresh restart. The director questioned if this was truly my plan and what I wanted. She suggested that I had the opportunity to start fresh right where I was and that I didn't have to run. "Yes, yes, I am going to be fine," I reassured her. "I don't belong here, this isn't my story," I repeated.

It's as if God gave me every opportunity to pause and listen to HIS plan for my life. I've heard so many times that the Christian walk is just to restrain us with a bunch of rules and regulations. No, my friend. Trust me when I say He is all about freewill.

> **While He will chase you down, it's simply to envelope you with His perfect love for you, not to restrain you.**

I'm sure His Father's heart wanted nothing more than to restrain me that day and plead with me to just trust Him enough to stop running. Yet, He allowed me to choose, and I allowed my fear to dictate my future.

The bus was bigger than I imagined it would be. Maybe it was the size of the dog running along the side of it that really baffled me. At this point, my life had been condensed to a duffle bag. I was exhausted and running on minimal sleep, desperate to just close my eyes and hoped they'd remain closed until we arrived in Minnesota.

The ride was horrendous, and I wondered if perhaps I should have taken the director's offer and started fresh from Tennessee. Multiple drug offers, three marriage proposals, and distasteful attempts to woo this nineteen-year-old girl led me to make a call to who, at this point, I was beginning to see as a savior.

I begged him to track the bus and pick me up somewhere in Wisconsin, anywhere that would get me off the bus sooner than planned. He did just that. I got off the bus and immediately started punching and slapping him, so angry that he would put me on a bus like that. Mike was about 6'3", blue eyes, short, thick, curly red hair, and mustache. He smelled like an ashtray masked with Axe body spray. I knew this would be the longest ride of my life. I was exhausted from the journey and starving for something deeper that a burger could never satisfy.

We finally made it to a little town called Byron. It would be home for the unforeseeable future, but I only expected it to be a few months. I would reconcile things with my parents and return to North Carolina, get my old job back, and start rebuilding a life I could be proud of.

I got my laptop set up at a desk prepared for me. It was placed in front of a window that overlooked the complex from the second floor of the two-bedroom townhome where we resided. I was anxious to connect with Mama LeeLee; I knew she'd be worried about me, and there was just something about her that was familiar. While I didn't know it then, she was the first, purest reflection of the Father's heart I had ever met. How could I feel so safe and protected by someone thousands of miles away? She was the home I truly longed for.

She also was not convinced I should have gone to Minnesota. She was bold and honest just as much as she was loving and compassionate. She was, however, convinced that Mike was not who he portrayed himself to be.

Merely a month went by, and we decided to venture out and explore the great state and attempt to count up these so-called 10,000 lakes. Let me just tell you, I am convinced they're counting ponds and puddles as lakes up there, and that's how they believe they have ten thousand. Anyway, I digress!

We took a walk in a nearby park through the woods, just talking through my plans, and I really started dreaming again. It was thrilling! I was most hopeful for restoration with my parents. Mike wandered off the path, lowered down through the trees. It was his plundering through the leaves and debris that made me turn my attention toward him. It was his posture that made my heart sink.

"Don't go, you already tried North Carolina. Now try Minnesota . . . it's just a matter of time before you're at odds with your parents again. Stay with me . . . marry me!" He pleaded. I stood there frozen, confused, trying to remember how to even breathe.

"Ummmm, I don't like you that way," I said. "I appreciate you rescuing me from my ex, but this is not the plan," I began to explain. He interjected, "You'll marry me or you won't make it out of these woods." I caught a glimpse of a younger guy coming up the trail, and it was as if Mike knew what my brain was processing. "Don't even think about it," he said.

"Yes, ok, I'll stay . . . I'll marry you," It had to have been my fear that uttered those words. While he celebrated as if this was some true love story, I forced a smile and wondered how in the hell I would get myself out of this one.

Mike was forty-six. I did not know if I would live to see twenty.

I still remember telling Mama LeeLee what was happening. I felt so much shame and disgust, yet with Mike a moderator in Worthy Chat, he had to be protected. He had me leave the chat all together and the only relationships that remained were those that move outside of those virtual walls.

Thankfully, Mama and I did most of our talking through Skype or by using a calling card and using my cell phone. She was the only one I felt I could trust.

He ran up the stairs with excitement and announced the day we would be married. While I've yet to erase the recording from my mind, I do not remember the date. How could we be going through the same experience so vastly different? My stomach turned as he rambled off the details. He had found a location, a pastor, my maid of honor, and I would be meeting his family for the first time . . . at our wedding.

I was so overwhelmed, everything was happening so quickly and I truly feared for my future. I remember it was in a park with a small body of water—it was probably one of the 10,000 lakes accounted for. I remember getting out of his low-riding white truck with a blue topper cover. He was a storm chaser, at least that was his hobby. His truck was covered with all sorts of crazy gadgets on top of the roof storm chaser vinyl down alongside the door on both sides.

I was petrified, I wondered what his family would think of me. Would they see my terror? Would they try to stop this madness that was quickly unraveling? They just looked at me with questions in their eyes, concern washed across their faces. There were two brothers, two sisters, and his parents. I just remember thinking how cute his parents were. His mom was so tiny standing next to his towering dad; it's as if I loved them instantly despite the situation at hand.

I saw a lovely, tall, blonde lady standing under a beautiful tree. I assumed that it was her husband beside her. She looked at me, smiled, and gave me an extended hug. "Hi, I am Betsy. I am your maid of honor. Honey, are you SURE you want to do this? You don't have to." She would become my only friend while in Minnesota. I felt the tears welling up in my eyes but all I could remember was what happened in the woods weeks prior. I swallowed hard, fearful of what would happen if I answered anything but yes.

> **She hugged me so deeply I was reminded of the times my God, my Father, had hugged me.**

Surrounded by strangers whose names I couldn't even recall, yet who were about to become my family, I wore a pair of Duckhead blue jeans, a green button-up shirt, and tennis shoes. We said our I do's, and then came the moment I had been dreading: the kiss. I felt repulsed, as if my life was ending rather than starting a new beginning filled with dreams and hopes for the future. After signing the papers on a picnic table, it was over as quickly as it had begun.

I was a virgin until this day, and I cherished my virginity more than life itself. It felt like the one thing in my life I had some control over. I don't recall ever having "the talk" about what it would be like when the time came. Perhaps with all the drama my family endured surrounding it, it was best left unspoken. Yet, here I was at twenty years old, terrified of what was about to happen. I didn't even know what love was, and I felt as though a piece of me was about to be stolen, with nothing I could do to protect it any longer.

We arrived back at our townhome, and he rushed upstairs, pulling me behind him. He seemed not to be wasting any time, unaware and uncaring of how I was processing all of this. There was a weak attempt to show care as he said, "We can go slow." The problem was, slow could never be slow enough to prepare my heart for the brokenness it was about to endure.

He stormed out of the room, frustrated and angry. I don't know if it was me gripping my last thread of dignity or my spirit simply refusing to allow it to happen. Either way, he was unable to penetrate all the way through. Just hours ago, he announced to his family his love for me, and now . . . there was nothing he hated more than me. I lay in that bed for what seemed like hours, lying in my own blood, in more pain than I had ever felt before, sobbing and wondering where my God was now.

His anger had to echo to our neighbors as he yelled of my ignorance and failure, slamming doors and grabbing a beer from the fridge. Storming up the stairs, he demanded I clean the mess I had made in his bed. He went into his office and slammed the door. I had to find the strength to get into the shower and wash myself of the indignity and shame. I would not be able to bathe long enough to ever make my soul feel pure again.

I went back to the bed and tried to silence my cries as I was forced to see just how bad it was. I pulled the sheets off the bed, not sure a washing machine could make them clean again. Desperate for my Father to hold me again, to pull me out of this misery, I believed I was too unclean for Him to ever hold me again. So, I went to the one that never failed to show me His heart, to remind me of my truth, Mama LeeLee.

I struggled to find words to explain the situation, knowing tomorrow would hold the same fate until he was satisfied. I tried to tell her what had happened. She gifted me with grace, and we just sat in the stillness of the night. Not a word had to be spoken, but I knew she was praying for me—praying that God would keep His protection on me and that I would find a way to turn my face back toward Him. We knew that would be a while, but she let me borrow her hope and faith until I could stand on my own again.

Eventually, I became numb to it all. It was an excruciating week of hell. I stopped fighting. I accepted this as my duty. I lost my value, my humanity. I was nothing more than a blow-up sex doll. All emotion had been removed. I learned to keep silent through the pain and escape into the darkest crevices of my mind.

Mama never pushed for details or even brought up the situation. It didn't need to be spoken. She knew. I feared she knew because of her own past that she never spoke of. I could see the tears in her eyes as we met for another Skype call. How graceful she was toward him when he would walk into view of the camera. While I was eternally grateful that she didn't antagonize him, both of our stomachs curdled with vomit that this is what had to happen to survive.

When I was with her, I could feel my Father wrap His arms around me. How could a woman in Manchester, England make me feel so safe? He had always sent someone to make His love tangible to me. I was the one that pushed Him away, I was the one that ignored the prompting of His Spirit. Yet, He still met me in the middle of my mess. It wasn't pretty. I didn't have the courage to even lift my face towards Him, but He was always there. It was just enough hope that I needed to plan my escape.

CHAPTER 7

Great Escape

Nearly six months had passed. I was so desperate to be truly loved and to love someone, I stopped taking my birth control and hoped God would give me a little one to love. I had found normalcy in my dysfunction. I drowned myself in worship and played it constantly.

I became a fan girl again, but instead of the Backstreet Boys, I was now following the ins and outs of Third Day. Did you know their fan base referred to themselves as Gomers and they had a forum and chat room called Gomertopia? Still makes me chuckle to this day . . . Gomers!

I wasn't consumed with the chat rooms as I had been in the past, but I did frequent them occasionally with the Gomers. It brought me the solace I was so desperate for.

I became really close with a family of Gomers from Texas. The Schnabels were kind and funny, and they loved real big! They led worship at church and just felt it deeper than I did. I was determined to learn how to get to that level. The family was beautiful inside and out.

My "adoption" just sort of happened. We went from friends to family over time, and while I was definitely skeptical after what happened in Tennessee, I saw it as perhaps the perfect escape route.

Mike and I worked out the details and planned to arrive on New Year's 2009. I wasn't completely honest with the family about my intentions for moving down.

I hoped God would give them eyes to see past my polished mask and the courage to free me from the hell I was living.

We pulled up to the old farmhouse, and it was actually freezing when we arrived. It didn't keep us from a joyous embrace in the driveway. The church where they led worship, The Ark, was literally in their backyard where breakfast was served every Sunday morning. We stayed up and talked for hours. I still remember the mom's smile; it illuminated the darkest parts of my soul that hadn't seen light in a long, long time.

It lasted until about June before we were asked to leave. Mike didn't care that we lived in someone else's home; I still had a duty to fulfill. I suppose my spirit was being exposed to just enough light to start to breathe life again.

For the first time, I told him no. The family was about to start a card game, and I wanted to play and be a part of their family game night. He erupted and stormed out of the house, but not before causing an uproar. I walked through the kitchen embarrassed and was stopped by the parents.

"Are you ok?" they asked. I was kind of shocked it took them this long to realize something was terribly wrong with our relationship. But they truly didn't judge anyone; they loved deeply. I told them what was happening, and this really upset the dad as he was a father of two girls of his own.

They fought for me more that night than I fought for myself my whole life. It was something in their eyes that transferred to my soul to rise up and claim, "You are worthy!"

The sheriff was called that night, and Mike was refused entrance to the house again. They sat me down and told me I could either go back to North Carolina, or I would have to go with Mike because I made a vow to take him as my husband. I was shattered to know my plan to escape was falling apart.

I unintentionally hurt a family I truly loved and cared deeply for. I was so consumed with my escape, I didn't think how he could potentially hurt those who would attempt to help me. My relationship with the Schnabels became strained. I carried that guilt for years until we could reconnect through social media, and I was able to apologize.

We moved out the next day into a duplex across town. I was working full time at Subway, still attending church at The Ark, and occasionally was allowed to go down to the coffee shop and hear "Gramps" sing. Gramps led worship at The Ark with the family we had stayed with. They were close friends that also became family.

Gramps had a favorite song he'd like to sing called "The Secret Place." I'd close my eyes and see myself by a waterfall, sitting in my Father's lap, my head pressed into His chest to hear His heart beat for me. It's the most beautiful harmony you'll ever hear.

Gramps was a good man, and Grammy, well, she too had a smile that illuminated the darkest places of my soul and breathed life back into my spirit.

It was the spring of 2009 when I found out I was pregnant. It was the first joy that I shared with Mike. But I didn't think about the life this child would have to overcome because of who her father would be, or how selfish her mom was to bring her into such a toxic and potentially fatal situation.

I was just two weeks into my pregnancy when God said, "Her name will be Savannah Grace." Three days passed, and He gave me a vivid dream of what she would look like, with her perfect complexion and the radiant glow I had seen in others along the way. It brought hope back to my spirit.

I shared this with some of my friends, and they just laughed and said, "It's just two weeks. What if you have a boy?" I was convinced God had given me a message and no one could convince me otherwise. There would be a great plan for her life, and I began praying that God would give her courage and that she would never live her life in fear as I had.

I didn't have much support in Texas. Many were pushed away by Mike, and with the news of me being pregnant, I was forced to quit my job. But I still had Grammy and Gramps. They made sure I got to church and had everything I needed to encourage a healthy pregnancy. Grammy would take me to the doctor for my appointments in Austin. This woman had a heart of gold. The only wrong she ever did with me was illegal U-turns to get back to the homeless so she could feed them and the stray dogs. She was a riot, alright. I believe they knew more of my story than anyone, yet I never had to say a single word.

We fell on hard times as I was not working and Mike lost his job. Money was running out, and so were our options. Mike told me to go ask Gramps and Grammy for money; they would surely give it to me. The light that had started shining again was starting to flicker. The conversation didn't go as we had planned. In fact, Gramps told us to get out of Texas and go back to Minnesota. I was so heartbroken and began to sob, sitting on their couch at a loss for words. My great escape just became an epic fail. We got in that old storm-chaser truck and started down their long dirt driveway. I couldn't understand why they were pushing me away.

I watched through the side mirror, praying that they would come running after me. I watched through that mirror until I could no longer see hope.

This night is often spoken about when I phone Grammy for our weekly chats, and only now is it understood I had an open invitation to stay. I am not even sure if I would have had the courage to stay in Texas had it been understood that night.

We started calling everyone we knew on the way back to Minnesota for help. Betsy would come back into my life as I shared the news of now being seven months pregnant. The celebration was cut short as I sheepishly asked if she could put us in a hotel for the night. He drove all night as far as he could. We slept in the truck in visitor centers until we made it to Iowa. He had a brother there that would give him money. It got us a motel room and I had an opportunity to secure my freedom.

We stopped to grab some cheap TV dinners before reaching the motel. Upon arrival, we were approached by a man, likely under the influence of drugs, wielding a metal pipe. Without warning, he began swinging the pipe at us. Mike instructed me to enter the room and leave the door cracked so he could follow. I hurried inside, placing the groceries on the dresser, and locked the door behind me. Trembling, I climbed into bed, hugged myself tightly, covered my ears, shut my eyes firmly, and prayed fervently for deliverance from the captivity I had endured for far too long.

The intensity of my prayers was interrupted by the banging on the door. "Why would you do that?" Mike exclaimed. He was upset that I had locked the door instead of leaving it cracked as instructed. I brushed it off as a mistake made in the heat of the moment, caught off guard by the traumatic events unfolding. Surprisingly, that was the shortest outburst he ever had. We managed to eat, get some rest, and the next morning, we headed for Rochester, Minnesota.

I found a doctor and scheduled an appointment right away, concerned for my baby girl given all the trauma we had been through, the lack of nutrition, and vitamins. Clinging to the promise God gave me, I sought to silence the lies running on repeat in my mind. So many times I came close to finding my freedom. I switched doctors frequently, receiving a new prescription each time as they began questioning my safety.

One doctor was bold enough to call it for what it was, stating that my symptoms were consistent with signs of rape and offering to help me. I often wondered if these people were part of God's army sent to rescue me. Yet, because it didn't look the way I thought it should, I missed it. Yes, I was scared, and I know that fear played a factor, but if the God of the universe sends His army out to rescue you, anyone that comes against you will not prosper. He promised it, and He keeps His word.

"Be still and know that I am God" (Psalm 46:10 NIV). It's in the stillness that God speaks. He prepares our hearts for what He is about to do, if only we would listen. He is waiting to give us our next step. That's right, the next step. Singular. I am convinced that if He were to have given me the full picture of what He was about to do, I would have never taken the next step.

> **As hard as it is not knowing all the details, it's in our obedience to the next step that our faith flourishes.**

We found a duplex in Rochester, where we lived above an elderly lady. If not for Betsy and the help of her church, I don't know where we would have ended up. They were our last hope. I'll never forget those stairs. There were at least a dozen steep stairs that led to our front door, which was more like a back door because of the layout. The door opened into the tiny kitchen with a small two-seater table. We had a living room, two bedrooms, and a bathroom.

Stepping into the bedroom to the left, I imagined what a nursery would look like. I cared about nothing else than my baby girl. I only had a couple of months left in my pregnancy, and I hoped I would feel a new, real love.

While Mama LeeLee and I would have seasons of silence, she remained close in my spirit. I connected with her soon after we settled in Rochester. It was the first time I told her of my pregnancy, and more than ever before, it made me long to have her with me in person.

I had been in communication with my parents as they too were not missed in Mike's desperate scouring for money from anyone who would help. I sensed their concern, yet also felt the silence as they were at a loss for words. How in the world could my life go so awry? It would take time, forgiveness, and unconditional love to mend our broken hearts.

I was seated at that little fold-out metal table, eating pasta, when it hit me. A sharp pain like never before gripped me, an intense ache that took my breath away. WHAT WAS THAT?! I called my mom and told her what was happening, and she said it was probably Braxton Hicks.

It was my Father's voice that sent me to the hospital that night. God spoke, "It's time, Tracey." I was no expert on His voice or interpreting Him by any means, but my spirit knew God meant there would be labor of different means coming my way.

It was December 29, 2009, around 5:45 pm. Ten-foot snow banks lined the sides of the road. What I feared most was getting down those dozen icy steps to make our way down the drive to the road where we parked. I fell over in the snow bank, trying to get my door to come loose from the frozen tundra. Another contraction was coming on, and so was another rampage from Mike . . . as if I asked to fall into the snow bank. I had one mission that night, and I had to stay focused on safely delivering Savannah, regardless of his outbursts.

We arrived at the hospital and were quickly given a room, and, glory to God, an epidural. Mike was irate as I was trying to follow the instructions of the nurses but terrified to have this needle go in my back and wondering what delivery would look like. I fell asleep after they successfully administered the epidural. I was already exhausted and had yet to even deliver my sweet girl. God reminded me of my dream and the vision of her face, and I was anxious to see if this truly was what my girl would look like.

Of course, she did! She was born approximately 1:26 am, and she was perfect. I was surprised to hear she was in perfect health. We struggled to breastfeed, giving us a few extra days in the hospital. Mike had so many outbursts that the nurses kept his visitations minimal. I was happy to spend extra days there.

The love I had hoped for I now held in my arms. I knew it wouldn't be easy, and I already found myself regretting bringing her into this chaos and nightmare, but I was determined to rescue both of us. After all, God had spoken, "It's time, Tracey."

Reverse Psychology

Four days had passed, and I was finally able to bring my baby girl home. She consumed me in a way that I forgot what home life was really like. All I felt was overwhelming love and joy that overflowed. I sat in the backseat with her on the way home, holding her hand the whole time. I had never felt a love quite like this.

I carried her up those treacherous stairs and welcomed her home, so excited to show her her room. I just wanted to take her out of her car seat and rock her in the rocking chair that had been given to us. "Hold up," he said, stopping us in the living room just twenty more steps to her room—where my world would dissolve of everything besides me and my baby girl. He continued, "If you ever attempt to leave with her, I will find you and I will be sure you never see her again. You can never call the police because they will take her from the both of us and you'll never see her again."

Suddenly, my joy was stiffened with his threats, but something inside of me believed every word. I knew from that day on she would never leave my sight. She would never be left with him alone.

It wasn't long before we moved out of that duplex and headed into another townhouse, where Mike took the job as property manager. It was a nice place; I called it little Russia because half of the tenants were Russians. Two bedrooms as before, but I was concerned as one was upstairs and the other was downstairs. While we made one a room for Savannah, it really was more of a playroom. I refused to sleep without her by my side.

Now, don't come at me with all your concerns of safety and how so many horrible things could have happened to her while co-sleeping. I am fully aware, and while I was concerned, it did not concern me nearly as much as the possibilities of what would happen if she slept alone downstairs.

Savannah brought so much joy; she was such a lil chunky monkey. She was full of curiosity and wonder. I was enthralled with her very being.

Her father, on the other hand, had little to do with her. There was the occasional game of peekaboo as long as it didn't interfere with his computer games. Not once did he ever change a diaper nor give her a bath.

He said that giving her a bath or changing her would just be inappropriate because she was female. If only he knew those were the words that empowered me to fight harder than ever for our freedom. It opened my eyes even more clearly to see we were both imprisoned by him and it was only a matter of time before he would make a move to steal her innocence as well.

Betsy continued to echo words of strength and encouragement: get out now while Savannah was still young. She wouldn't remember these first years, and the longer we waited, the worse things would get. It was crazy to think that this twenty-one pound child would strengthen me and give me the courage to finally make my move. I was reminded of the words of my Father, "it's time, Tracey." Indeed, it was time.

I tried to get help from local resources for victims of domestic abuse. Since I did not have any physical marks, broken skin or hospital stays, there was nothing they could do for me. How does that even make any sense? I pleaded with the director and tried to find logic in what she was saying. I even told her that he had people watching me. If I was caught coming out of that building I would be killed and they'd be doing an autopsy on me when they could simply rescue me now. None of it made sense.

I was advised to record his outbursts and threats, BUT I would have to ask his permission before recording him or it would not be legal. What in the world is wrong with our system? Did they know what I had to do to even get the courage to come here today? I endangered my neighbor and family by asking them for a ride. As the property manager, Mike could have retaliated and kicked them from their home for helping me if he ever found out.

I was so disheartened and disappointed that this . . . this was the land of the free and home of the brave. Yet, it wasn't for me.

I started sharing with my parents what life was really like in Minnesota, how I never wanted to be here, and how I needed to escape and find a safe place for me and Savannah. I would secretly call them, hiding my phone within the couch so they could hear his rage.

We began having discussions as to what coming back home to North Carolina would look like. I didn't care about the stipulations that were put in place. We were reaching the point of life and death. It could be felt in the atmosphere.

> **Despite the cyclone of fear, shame, regret, depression, and hopelessness that was swirling around, I could still feel my Father.**

Savannah was now six months old, and I knew I would have to manipulate him the way he had done to me for so many years. I settled down and began to make him feel I really loved him, cared for him. This required making sacrifices and taking my "duties" as his wife to a new level of shame and despair.

I submitted quicker than ever before, afraid to have Savannah left downstairs alone. I prayed that God would protect her in every way and let this pass quickly. I was willing to do anything to expedite our freedom and then focus on my healing later.

My plan was working. His raging fits decreased the more I submitted to him. I was in so much pain from having to do "double duty" but with our freedom on the horizon, I knew I had no choice but to push through it all.

I started discussions with Mike about moving to North Carolina. It was my homeplace, and since he wasn't close to his family, we could move closer to mine. We could restore what was fractured, have help with Savannah, and both find work and a home of our own.

I encouraged this for a couple of months before changing the script ever so slightly to Savannah and I would go ahead to North Carolina and get a lay of the land. I would start work, look for a home, and find a property management job for him as well. Within a few months he would be able to join us and we'd be starting our new lives! Oh, those years of theater class were paying off!

I finally got him to agree sometime around December 2010. I thought I had it all figured out. It was working perfectly!

We agreed to celebrate Savannah's birthday there in Minnesota and invite his family. It was hard knowing that just days later, Savannah and I would board a plane and never return to the state of Minnesota. I had to remind myself constantly that they didn't know the hell we were living in, and if they did, I had to believe they would help us escape.

As I waited patiently for my parents to arrange the airline tickets, I began to see our freedom just peek above the horizon! God gave me my next step through my mother's boss: Write an agreement, have him sign it, notarize it and THEN you can leave.

I really battled with God on this one. He was about to blow up my whole plan, six months of planning and the things I had to submit to just to get his "yes" to let me go. I feared having this agreement would make him suspect that there was something else going on, and he would take back everything.

> **My Father wrapped His arms around me like only He could do and whispered, "Trust me."**

I didn't trust anyone. So many had failed me. Those I should have been able to trust, proved that I couldn't. Mike had me so paranoid that everyone was watching me, including his friends in Hell's Angels. I trusted no one except Betsy and my neighbor.

"Trust Me." He continued to whisper this until my spirit submitted to His Spirit. Yes, "submit"—a word that, to this point in my life, only harmed me and brought me great pain that would take years to undo and heal from.

But this was my Father . . . the One that was always there. The One, that if I took a moment and looked back, I could see His hand every step of the way. My life was evidence of His faithfulness. How could I possibly not trust Him now in such a critical moment?

I wrote up the agreement myself, adding every pertinent detail I could think of, allowing God to guide my hand with every stroke of the keys. I took it jokingly to Mike, saying, "Hey, let's sign this together and notarize it so we know this is legit and there is no going back." I never added anything about Mike joining us later or me ever returning to Minnesota if things didn't work out—it was strictly my letter to freedom.

I'll never know if he didn't actually read it or take it seriously, or if God added a few lines for only his eyes to see, but he agreed. We went down to our bank and signed it on January 4, 2011, and three copies were made: one for him, one for me, and one secretly given to my neighbor, just in case he took mine in the night.

I was set to board a plane at MSP on January 6, 2011.

On January 5, 2011, I just had to keep Savannah and myself safe for twenty-four more hours and we would be free. Everything started out just fine. I had our bags packed, my letter tucked away in my bag hidden among my clothes, and I was ready. I started preparing our last dinner together, and that's when everything changed.

It all happened so quickly. Before I knew it, I was pinned against the kitchen counter, and he just stared into my soul. Never had I seen such darkness in anyone's eyes, including my sister's from long ago. As vile and horrid as Mike was, who he became in that moment was something far worse, and I feared that even he did not have control of what was to come.

With his nose nearly touching mine, he grabbed the butcher knife from the block behind me and said, "You won't make it on that plane. Hell's Angels are coming for you, and I will have Sav all to myself." He went downstairs and out the door to the garage. I ran and wrapped my baby girl in my arms, clinging to her with the last ounce of strength I had and called my mother.

We had rehearsed this just in case. All I could do was whisper 911 repeatedly. But I was sobbing and hyperventilating between each number I whispered. I crouched against the wall in the fetal position, my baby girl clenched to my chest. What if he was right? What if the police would take my little girl?

I heard him yell through the garage, and his voice echoed into our home, "THEY WON'T MAKE IT, NICE TRY." This was a new evil I had never before encountered. There was NO WAY he could have heard me. My mother relayed questions from the police: "Are there any weapons?" He answered the questions himself while still in the garage, "I HAVE A GUN AND I TOOK THE BUTCHER KNIFE." It made it more abundantly clear. I had found myself right in the middle of another holy war.

I was losing hope that we would make it out alive. If the police did not show in the next few minutes, we would surely be killed, at least I would be. They charged through the door onto the landing and started making their way up the stairs where I sat, my baby girl still clenched against my chest.

"Don't take my baby, please don't take her from me. I am sorry. I am trying to escape. Just don't take her from me. I can keep her safe," I pleaded over and over again. The officers quickly got a glimpse into what kind of life we must have been living. They tried to assure me, but it still took about twenty minutes for me to calm down and trust that they would keep us safe.

They assured me that they were not there to take my baby, rather to help us get to safety. They said, "Whatever he has told you is a lie. We're not going to hurt you. In fact, we're not even going to touch you or your baby. We'll take your bags. We just need to get you out of here."

The officers asked me where they could take me, and all I could think to say was my neighbor. So they took me out the back door and in through the neighbor's back door where we stayed all night.

I never knew what happened to Mike that night; I didn't care. I just prayed that Savannah wouldn't cry out in the night and risk him knowing where we were hiding. We left for the airport before the break of dawn the next morning. I had never been more scared in my life. I continued to hear his threats of how I wouldn't make it on the plane—how Hell's Angels would be watching me. My neighbor could only take me so far, and then it was just me and my baby girl. Several tried to help, and I just kept fighting.

I still remember walking down that long corridor and seeing my parents for the first time in nearly five years. I remember their embrace. I remember my first exhale and how the tears poured out. I know I must have looked like a crazy person in the airport that day, but everyone saw the anguish on my face. God gave me the courage to trust one man who carried my bags, as I carried Savannah in her car seat. I remember breathing in freedom and thanking God for the next step.

CHAPTER 9

Coming Home

On January 7, 2011, I expected to wake up full of hope, embracing my freedom. But that's just not how it happens, though. Freedom would have to be fought for, and this was just day one of that battle.

I didn't know at the time the vulnerability and courage it would take to claim my freedom from the hell I had been living. Words couldn't describe the joy I felt waking up with my baby girl in my arms and yet no sign of him.

"It's just you and me now, kiddo. We're safe now."

Unfortunately, laws kept me captive to Mike, despite having over 1,200 miles between us. He'd call, sometimes multiple times a day, completely delusional about the traumatic departure he put us through. He was still fully convinced I was here to start a new life and he'd be joining us in a few months.

I didn't have the courage yet to tell him that was never going to happen. I allowed fear to become the warden of my life, and it left me imprisoned for many years to come.

I wasted no time looking to piece my life together. Rather quickly, I found a church—it was the Mickey hands that drew me in, but it was the people that made me stay. I had dreams of having my own home to raise Savannah, complete with an oak tree and tire swing for a good measure of fun.

I didn't finish college, and as a single mom, I didn't feel I had the time to think about school. So I went back to the only thing I knew—flipping burgers. I worked hard, thinking that perhaps if I worked hard enough, I could at least move up to management and find a way to get out on my own.

My parents helped me obtain my license again; it had been nearly six years since I had driven a car. They also helped me get a car of my own since I had no work history. I couldn't get a loan; my parents had to purchase the car, and I made payments to them until it was paid in full.

I was approved for assistance to take Savannah to daycare, and thankfully, there was one right behind my work.

Nothing prepares you for the fear and anxiety of dropping your baby off at a new place with strangers, hoping they will love them even half as much as you do. Add three years of complete paranoia and constant reminders that you are being watched and Hell's Angels are coming for you—needless to say, drop-offs took longer than expected.

I am thankful for their patience and understanding, even though they didn't know my story. They created space for grace in my circumstance, updating me throughout the day and even coming by my work at lunchtime to give updates and show me pictures.

That's God—intentional focus on the intricate details of your life that you didn't even know existed. He lavishes His love on His children and calls them His beloved.

> **His one desire is for you to know how deeply loved and fully known you truly are.**

My parents began to charge me rent, which I could understand and appreciate for the core values they were trying to instill, but I could never seem to find myself getting ahead. I wasn't drinking or partying—I was a mom now, and that is a whole new level of responsibility. I worked, came home, cleaned the house, and spent whatever time I had left loving my baby girl.

Things were a bit different as my parents had also adopted my sister's firstborn. She always reminded me of a Precious Moments doll with her curly blonde locks, eyes of blue, and tiny dimples. I knew she was far better off with my parents than ever a day with my sister. But I also saw the toll it all took on my parents. They weren't as young as they used to be. They were weary from this life. They spent so many years just trying to piece this family back together in hopes that it would look the same as it did before the spring of '98.

In July 2011, we were ordered to attend court in Minnesota. I tried to plead my case that I was a single mom with a one year old—could I not just join by phone? I explained the danger of the situation, but it didn't matter. I had to be in person, although they would provide me with security when I arrived. It was time to finally bring that season to an end. I would do whatever was required to break free from him.

Thankfully, my mom went with me to Minnesota. We arrived at the courthouse and immediately had security assigned to us. I still remember the fear and paranoia that enveloped me as I walked down the long, unoccupied hallways, terrified that he would be waiting and hiding in one of these rooms. I was so full of fear, I didn't even want to leave Savannah alone with my mom. What if it was a trap? What if they were harmed or kidnapped while I was in the courtroom?

> **We're quick to personify our enemy—it must be someone. But what if it's something? What if fear is our greatest enemy, and we miss defeating it because we confuse if for somebody?**

I entered the courtroom with my manila folder full of emails and text messages—over a hundred pages of conversations filled with threats and fear-induced manipulation. I was prepared to fight for my baby girl, to fight for myself, to fight for our freedom. While it appeared to the judge and others in the room that I was alone, I knew my Father was standing right beside me, reminding me that He would continue to protect me.

I was so fearful that I couldn't even look at Mike standing at the podium just twenty feet away from me. I just wanted it over so

I could hold my baby girl and know she was safe. "She kidnapped her, your honor. I want them ordered to move back to Minnesota immediately!" Was that possible? Wait, kidnapped? I WAS THE ONE KIDNAPPED!

I knew it was the presence of my Father that kept me calm, assuring me He would handle this. The judge questioned me and made me aware of the serious accusations. "No, ma'am, your honor. We signed an agreement that I had notarized." The officer was instructed to get my paper for the judge—the agonizing wait. I catch a glimpse of him—a smirk across his face as though he would walk out in victory, overpowering me again.

The judge looked up and made us confirm these were our true signatures. "Yes, but she wrote that herself on the computer, there was no lawyer involved," he retorted. The judge looked at me and questioned what made me write this paper. I explained briefly the life we lived and I needed to protect myself and my daughter, and this is the plan God gave me. "You're a smart young lady, I could have ordered you back to Minnesota today, this was your saving grace," said the judge.

"Next matter . . . custody," the judge declared. "You'll both have to undergo psychological evaluations, there'll be supervised visitation for each of you one-on-one with Savannah . . . " the judge continued in our next steps, but I heard none of it. Why would they allow my baby with him alone? I told them we weren't safe.

"NO, I AM NOT DOING THAT . . . she can have her!" Mike exclaimed with panic, knowing his truth would soon come to light.

"Case closed, you are granted full physical custody and can go back to North Carolina to reside."

Five minutes . . . that was it. . . . Five minutes and it was over just like that. I urged her to look at my chat logs I brought. Does not him refusing the evaluation speak volumes? "Oh it does, but it's over . . . go home," the judge urged.

I stood in disbelief; the officer led me back to my baby girl. I held her tighter than ever before and just cried. Unfortunately, I was still required to let Mike spend three hours with her before we left, but I was allowed to stay with her and our old pastor was the mediator. I was three hours from freedom . . . at least for the most part. It was years before Mike stopped his harassments and threats. As far as I know, he still lives somewhere in Minnesota.

My parents and I didn't always see eye to eye. In fact, I often felt as though my parents could never understand who I was. How the scars from my story had molded me into someone they had never met before. They tried to love me for who I was, not realizing I was a very, very different person. I am more broken now than ever before. My past left me trusting no one and skeptical of anyone who said they loved me.

I was desperately trying to pick up the pieces of my own life and I didn't want them to feel responsible for my mess as well. So, I left. I went to the one no one would ever expect. One that will leave you gasping and wondering what type of desperation could push one to go back to where the pain all began.

I followed that old gravel path, dodging the rough terrain created from the weather for what seemed like hours, contemplating over and over again . . . "What the hell are you doing?" I pulled up alongside the popup camper parked in the backyard of some friends. I unbuckled Savannah from her car seat and looked up towards the camper. I forced a smile as our eyes met, "Welcome home, sis!"

Savannah and I would spend the next unforeseen future on the pullout sofa of this camper while my sister took the only bedroom. The landlord had three kids, one being a little girl that became Savannah's best friend, her first friend. I became friends with her mom and she was a safe place for me to share my story. She was just as shocked as you are to see me living with my sister again.

I struggled with nightmares quite often. I found myself paranoid, and the longer time went on, the more intense these feelings became. With Savannah gone most of the time and sleeping at the landlord's house most nights, I became desperate to numb the pain any way I could. PTSD paranoia episodes would start and I'd find myself pinching myself until I bruised or clawing myself with my nails, or simply pressing my nail into my forearms until I could focus on the physical pain more than the mental torment playing out in my mind.

This was a new form of abuse I wasn't used to. It was dark and deep. While I knew full well that I was sitting in a camper in North Carolina, my mind was convinced I was in Minnesota hiding from Mike and his "gang." I began to drink with an intensity sending me into a drunkard coma and part of me hoped I'd never wake up again.

The velocity at which her foot made an impact with my stomach nearly made me barf. "Hey, HEY WAKE UP!" my sister's yelling woke me from my slumber. I looked up at her standing over top of me, laughing. I saw the liter of Smirnoff bottle beside me and guilt flooded me. How could I be so stupid? I couldn't move, the room was spinning and I could barely focus on my sister's face. "See, you're no better than me after all," she said laughing as she left, leaving me on the camper floor.

I woke up the next morning with a massive headache, still on the camper floor trying to make sense of where I was—more importantly where my baby girl was. I ran out of the camper screaming for her to come out wherever she was. Had she run away? Had she been taken from me due to one stupid night of regret? I frantically ran to the landlord's front door, banging on the door and pleading for them to open up. They did, but they wouldn't let me enter. They reassured me quickly that Savannah was fine; she had run to their home the evening before and they assumed it was fine she stayed the night as she had so many times before. I told them what happened and how I screwed up but this wasn't me . . . this wasn't my story.

Yes, I didn't quite see the pattern as quickly as you can now, but there was most definitely a pattern in my life. Those I surrounded myself with. The messes I created. The same ol' phrases . . . this isn't my story. So desperate to write my fairytale without all the heartache.

My landlords were having a hard time with my sister. It seemed as though she was trying to mess around with the husband, and the wife had had just about enough. I apologized for my part and my sister's and hated that I was reliving my past all over again. I had to get out. They tried to bargain with me and said, "No, you stay. We'll kick her out. You can have the camper and you pay whatever you want . . . we just want your sister gone far from here. Last night does not define you. You slipped up, and we'll help you get sober again."

> **"Last night doesn't define you." Some of the most powerful words that were ever spoken to me.**

Your addiction doesn't define you. Your self-harm doesn't define you. Your temporary lapse in judgment, DOESN'T DEFINE YOU! Remember when you were a child? You would draw pictures and give them to your parents, teachers, relatives, whoever. What would nearly always be asked next? "Aww thank you, what did you draw?" Of course, always in the sweetest tone and empowering manner as if you'd be the next Picasso. It was your creation, so only you could define what it is you had created. It's the same way with God . . . He created each and every one of us and ONLY He can define what each of us are. Created for a divine purpose only YOU can fulfill.

As tempting as it was to take them on their offer, I was yet again on the run. They knew of the alcohol. They didn't know I had found myself in a new kind of chat room and just how quickly I was about to hit my rock bottom.

CHAPTER 10

Rock Bottom

I think it was living with my sister again that convinced me I was simply meant to live a life of pain. Perhaps the few were right; I deserved it. After all, everywhere I found myself, I was living some sort of abuse. It couldn't be coincidence; it had to be my fate. The names in this next chapter have been changed to protect the identities of those involved and their families.

Submissive - one ready to conform to the authority or will of others; meekly obedient or passive.

That's what I had become before I even knew it was a title to be held. Despite everything I had been through, I still underestimated the darkness to be uncovered through the world of Google. I found a whole community of people that, like me, felt as if they deserved to be punished for every wrong they did. I found a select few that had the exact mindset as myself. If I was going to be abused everywhere I went in this life, I might as well accept it to give myself even a false delusion that I had some control over what was happening to me.

Dominate - most important, powerful, or influential.

Aunt Linda was her name. Colombian descent, long black hair; there was just something about her that made you know not to cross her. She once called the Triangle home but was moving to New York for work. I picked her up from the RDU airport when she came back to move more of her things, but not before I decked my car out as the Smurf mobile, yet again teasing her about her short stature. It was as though I went back to a younger version of myself to live out my childhood that was stolen from me. We had a good laugh, but she warned me I would soon regret such banter.

We had our first session, as she called them, in an apartment up in Virginia Beach, as I took her to Virginia to see her dad. I was nervous. While I wasn't so nervous about the pain I would soon endure, I battled with shame I knew would break through the floodgates if I allowed this all to unfold. I had entered the world of spankos and never realized until I left the lifestyle how deep, dark, and twisted it really was. Yet, at the end of every session, I waited for the words, "I love you," served with Menchies frozen yogurt or hot chocolate and a cookie from Tim Hortons. This was now what love was. Love was pain. To be loved was to be pained.

I called my best friend from high school and asked her to take a road trip with me to New York to help me move my stuff there. Of course, she was on board. It nearly cost us our friendship, though, once we got stuck in an apple orchard somewhere in Pennsylvania. Needless to say, we can talk about anything in our friendship, including why I went, but we NEVER talk about the road trip to get there. I pray you find yourself a friend as solid as C-Moore. No judgment, all love. We don't talk nearly as much as we'd like to, but when we do . . . it's like a day hasn't passed. We went to explore Niagara Falls the next day before she headed back to North Carolina. Savannah is still convinced there are purple dolphins in Niagara Falls, thanks auntie C-Moore.

The next day I met Jordan. She was a part of the lifestyle as well, and she became a big part of my life and a security for me while I was there. I called her sister, but I realized it was different with her. Perhaps because she came in after the damage my biological sister left on me. I would just fight her for no reason. Don't worry 'bout Jordan, she was fine. She was a big ol' teddy bear, and I was safe in her arms. Apparently she had an intense pain tolerance, and my feeble attempt to fight her was merely felt and, if it ever was, she made sure to make me aware of it. I can't explain it . . . it was just the oddest thing. It's as though she became my punching bag and my chance at revenge for all the years my biological sister put me through. While I wish I would have handled that one a lot better, I am thankful that she was bold enough to be that for me. No wonder my girls still love her to this day.

While Savannah moved to New York with me, she had no idea why we were there. As crazy as our life had been, it unfortunately was becoming normal for her to move often. I was there with only one agenda, to fully step into this lifestyle I'd found. Our sessions were nearly always held at a hotel, or in their basement while Uncle Kaleb took the kids to Chuck E. Cheese . . . again. Savannah was making friends. I found work selling software for school testing and I became completely unaware of the world outside of this life I was living.

It's crazy just how fast brokenness can suck you in and blindside you before you even realize what is happening.

> **We're ALL broken, we're human. It's what we do with that brokenness that will determine the outcome of our lives.**

Will we succumb to our brokenness, or will we allow it to be the space for a seed to be sewn and God's love to water it and become something beautiful?

It was in New York that I started seeing a therapist and was diagnosed with PTSD paranoia. Finally, an answer for the night terrors, paranoia, and moments that I would escape reality and be fully convinced I was running for my life in Minnesota. As terrible as PTSD paranoia is, I found myself relieved that there was an answer for my madness. Unfortunately, it wasn't before it made scars on my forearms. I started on medication right away. I only remember one was for sleep, one for anxiety, and the other to keep the paranoia episodes at bay. It did more than that . . . it kept me at bay. I was a single mom and while I was with a family that helped me, I couldn't be a mom to Savannah while on this medication. I went from one world of manic chaos to one unaware and everything moving in slow motion. It was just awful. I took it for about a month and while it definitely helped, I had decided I couldn't live my life like this anymore. But taking my medication was one of the rules Aunt Linda had put in place, and as someone who was going to school to be a doctor, she took it very seriously.

I got tired of her asking me if I took my medicine, so I finally came clean. Told her I stopped taking it because I didn't think the side effects made it worth it. Moments later our room was booked and I was told to prepare myself. I got in the car and not a word was spoken. I believe it really was the most fearful thing about Aunt Linda. It was calm before the storm.

I kept my focus outside the passenger window the whole time, unable to recognize any of my surroundings and just how far we were going away this time. I wondered if she was intentionally trying to egg on an episode for me. There was just something different about this night and I knew it.

We pulled up to this sketchy motel. Potholes the size of craters, the men standing outside smoking cigarettes leaning against their old Ford trucks. She turned off the car and said, "These men are about to hear you all night, I hope they didn't come expecting sleep." She wasn't usually this theatrical . . . something was very, very different.

While there was never anything remotely sexual associated with what was happening, we still had a safe word in case the punishment had truly gone too far. I was ordered to grab my bag and to grab her bag of implements that would soon be used to bruise my backside and thighs. My hands were sweaty as I obeyed her commands. The men bid us a good night as we entered our room.

As I went to the bathroom I heard the clanking of her paddles and bath brushes. I feared the cherry oak paddle with holes the most. When I came out of the bathroom, a chair was in the middle of the room. This was new. I'd heard it intensified everything, and I began to wonder if I should just run and take my chances at finding my way back home alone in the dark. But there was no escape. She wasted no time, and before I knew it, we were a good twenty minutes into beating and scolding about how selfish and reckless I was to just stop my medication.

There would be a reprieve as I was told to stand in the corner, although this wasn't for me. This was truly for her to find rest before she went another round on me. Again she started, giving twenty to thirty swats before switching to another implement. I began to feel blood running down my thigh, trying to block with my hand, but knowing good and well it too would be swatted away.

"RED . . . RED!!" I began to plead, "please stop. I'm bleeding."

She didn't care. It was as though she was in another world herself. It was everything I could do to keep myself bent over the chair so the paddle wouldn't hit my spine.

All I could hear was my sobbing and the door closing. She was gone. I assumed she went to smoke and would soon return. She had never gone this hard on me before, and never had it ever ended without a discussion, hugs, and of course, "I love you."

I lowered my body to the floor, trying to see the damage she had caused. I was still bleeding, though some had already dried on my thighs. I lay on the floor for quite a while, just sobbing and thinking of what just happened and how I got to this place in my life. I'd replaced alcohol and self harm with true affliction. This was an all-time low.

As I looked at the blood on my hand I thought of the Man who was beaten for me.

"No, don't YOU come here. Don't YOU meet me in this motel room." I pleaded harder for Jesus to leave me there in that room alone than I did for Aunt Linda to stop my punishment.

He took my face in His hands and said, "My child, I endured this so you wouldn't have to. I AM love."

I went to clean myself up the best I could. I could barely get my pants on. I was already so swollen. We went home that night, as usual. But not a word was spoken. No frozen yogurt. No cookies or hot chocolate.

> **Just the words of my Father echoing His love for me.**

Why would He still meet me in such an awful place? It was my choices that got me there. He had already rescued me so many times and yet here I am still messing everything up and yet He's right there in the middle of it with me. I had never met a love like this before. Of course I knew Jesus, knew His love, but I was experiencing a new depth of His love tonight.

We snuck in the house in the wee hours of the morning sometime after midnight. Everyone asleep besides Linda and me . . . still other than her cold words of shame and disgrace for me earlier, not a word had been spoken. She went her way and I went mine. Nothing was ever the same between us after that. I went to my bed and grabbed this pink, five-foot sock monkey with lanky arms and legs. I threw its arms around myself and begged God to rescue me once more. I knew I had to get us out of New York and back to North Carolina. I asked Him to come into my room now, since I wasn't all exposed like in that motel room. Come to me now God, come hold me now. I am desperate to feel your touch. I wept silently hoping to not wake anyone. Just as I felt myself dozing off, my door creaked open.

She never said a word. It was as if she didn't hear my directives to go back to her bed. She had already been given a directive by her heavenly Father and she was following it ever so precisely. She climbed into my bed and wrapped her arms around me, never uttering a word. Some would call it coincidence, but you'll never convince me otherwise. While it certainly looked like my four-year-old, freckled face, red-headed daughter . . . I knew it was ultimately my Father holding me in His arms that night.

The next morning, I questioned Savannah as to why she came to my room last night and why wouldn't she go back to bed when I asked her to. She remembered nothing, she was convinced she stayed in her bed all night. While she was in her bed in the morning, I knew she had her arms wrapped around me until I fell asleep. God doesn't discriminate. He doesn't care your age or the color of your skin, your past, or present . . . all He needs is a willing vessel. All He needs is your "yes!"

Things were never the same in the house after that night. We didn't talk about it. I knew it was time to go back home. It was time to stop running from my past and brokenness and start running INTO His loving arms. It was time to chase Him down as He had done for me so many times. I went down to the basement to get away from the noise to see if God would show me the way back to North Carolina. I turned on my worship music and invited Him in. I didn't expect to find myself in yet another spiritual war.

I felt darkness, but there weren't any shadows this time. To be honest, I suppose it could have been another PTSD paranoia episode and the result of abruptly stopping my medication. "Just kill yourself now and be done with it, you'll never rise from this shame anyways, it will consume you, you are filth this is your final failure." I was terrified, this was a spiritual war I had never fought before. How was he taunting me with worship playing? I thought that was the key to make them flee.

There was a chair and a rope in the middle of the room. "Just do it you worthless fool!" How did my Father hold me the night before and now He's nowhere to be found and our enemy is the only one in the room with me. I fought for words to fight back with but just as in the house off of 95, I was frozen with fear. I closed my eyes and said His name in my mind over and over again until they became audible. It felt as though I had been born deaf and mute and was all of a sudden finding words to speak for the first time. The only word I could find was JESUS . . . JESUS . . . JESUS!!!

While I couldn't see the darkness tormenting me . . . I heard him screech in agony at the sound of HIS name. I heard the anger rise in his voice, now questioning for himself how this could be happening.

"JESUS . . . JESUS . . . JESUS," I knelt on the floor rocking back and forth until the only thing I heard was the sound of my Father's name and Chris Tomlin singing a praise . . . "I called your name, you heard my cry. Out of the grave, and into life. My heart is yours, my soul is free. Thank you God for saving me. Thank you God for saving me. Thank you God for saving me."

I found the courage to finally look up. The chair and rope I once saw in the middle of the room were gone. I ran upstairs, into the kitchen where Uncle Kaleb was making dinner. "Where's Savannah? I am sorry I was down there so long . . . I couldn't begin to explain what I had just experienced. I doubt they'd believe me anyway."

"So long?" he said, "it was only like fifteen minutes." I was even more confused. It felt as though I had been down there for hours fighting my enemy. I was exhausted. "Kaleb, you have to help us get out of here, I have to go back to North Carolina as soon as possible," I pleaded. He simply replied with an "okay" as though North Carolina was merely right across town.

I put in my two weeks' notice, and my boss released me early in the kindest way. "You're a sweet girl with a heart to serve, but you are the worst salesperson I have ever met. Safe travels home," he said. We just laughed, and I thanked him for giving me a shot at least and for not firing me sooner, since now I really knew how he felt about me.

We would load the minivan and my car the next morning and move in with a family friend, the single father of my sister's third child. With my sister gone in the wind again, surely I could piece my life back together despite the circumstances.

CHAPTER 11

Settling Down

We moved into the trailer off Cornwallis Rd. It wasn't much, but it was the safest we had felt in a long time. It was a packed house—Jack, two of his daughters, his cousin, and now Savannah and myself were joining the three-bedroom packed home. Savannah and I took the last bed available, the pull-out couch. Somehow we made it work, and we were happy. Savannah became best friends with Jack's youngest, who was technically Savannah's cousin, but given the chaos and brokenness of our family, they really hadn't spent much time together until now. Jack and I really got along well and understood each other on a deeper level as single parents.

While there was security and peace in the house, it was still just a house full of broken people looking to each other to glue us back together. I went back to work again doing the only thing I really knew—flipping burgers. I worked the night shift, came home, and cared for the kids, and didn't go to sleep until they went down for naps. Jack worked days and cared for the girls at night. It was exhausting but we somehow made it work.

It wasn't long before Jack started making bold statements, "I'm gonna marry you one day."

"Oh no kind sir, taking care of my sister's child while not being convinced she is yours is admirable . . . but I am done with that dating life much less marriage."

If he wanted a relationship with me, he'd first have to solidify his relationship with Christ. If God wanted me with him, He'd have to make it abundantly clear, because I was done screwing up my life.

It took a while before he came around and wanted to see what the "Mickey hands" were all about. But it wasn't long after stepping into that family of faith that he too started serving every Sunday with me.

I started seeing my parents more often and saw hope of restoration for my family, at least with my parents. We still didn't see eye to eye on everything and I didn't feel confident I could even share my story with them without being condemned. I did what everyone told me to do. The past is the past . . . move on.

We decided to take a family vacation together, ALL of us, including Jack and his youngest. It felt like old times, Myrtle Beach, laughs, sandcastles and the occasional bickering just for old time sake. Jack and I decided to get brave and go parasailing. I was terrified we'd be eaten by sharks, and he enjoyed making fun of me every time we were dipped into the water. You know what they say don't you? Conquering fears together draws people closer together . . . it just happened. Still flying high in the sky and that's where we had our first kiss, soaring over the Atlantic.

For once, the holidays seemed to pass by slowly . . . but I won't be mad at it. We rang in the New Year and navigated our way through Valentine's Day (I am not a fan). Resurrection Sunday was upon us. Of course, we were serving a long day at church. We celebrated Easter later in the day with Easter dinner at my parents' house, and then made our way back home.

There had been some shifts in the home and I now had a room. There on my bed was an Easter basket for me. While I was twenty-seven years old, it made me smile and feel loved. I was exhausted from the day and just wanted to rest. I was on a phone call and Jack kept texting me to see if I had started opening my eggs yet.

"NO DUDE! What's the big deal? I am not hungry for anything right now."

His persistence annoyed me to just open the eggs to see what was there and thank him for his efforts. Then it all made sense . . . inside one of the eggs was an engagement ring and a sweet note, obviously ending in "Will you marry me?" I stayed in the room for a LONG time talking to Jesus . . . and freaking out.

I reconnected with Mama LeeLee. I had a lot to catch her up on; it had been far too long since we last spoke. She was battling with her health; diabetes is a crippling disease. I worried for her, and being across the seas, it made it so much harder. My heart broke for her as much as hers broke for mine as I confided in her about New York. She never judged, never pushed or scolded. Always loved me through it all. At least I could follow it up with some good news. In my heart, this would be my first marriage. It was different. It was love.

Two months later, June 2014, we married sooner than expected at the church where we served. Given our circumstances, two blended families trying to blend together . . . we needed to go through counseling and we really weren't in a rush to get married. But we were told we needed to marry or one of us needed to move out immediately. Moving out wasn't an option, so we felt forced to go ahead and get married the following Sunday after service and trusted that we would still work through the counseling. Unfortunately, we never heard back from the countless times we asked for counseling from the church. We had God; that would be enough right?

After our first anniversary, I got a doozy of a surprise. It was then that I found out what I thought was his first marriage was actually his second and I was his third. Also, there were two more kids from the first marriage. It was a gut punch. I was angry to say the least. I thought I had found a place of trust and security. All of a sudden, nothing felt secure . . . yet again. I prayed—a lot. Divorce was not an option; Lord knows I had a past myself. I chose forgiveness, but even as I write these words, I question if I ever truly did. If I truly forgave him, would I have spiraled back to old habits?

I logged in to the spanko world . . . just to see what would happen. I saw some old familiar names and my experience with Aunt Linda had gotten out. I was picked up pretty quickly by one of the biggest names in the lifestyle, we'll just call her Big Mama. She wanted to assure me that what I experienced was not the "right way," and she wanted to prove that to me.

My husband knew of this part of my life. He may not have understood the ins and outs of it all, but he wanted me happy, whatever that looked like. There was an event happening within this lifestyle and I was invited to join them in Indiana. We booked a plane ticket, and I planned to go. After all, it couldn't have been any worse than what I had already experienced.

When you're with one of the biggest names in the business, you can rest assured that you'll have the VIP treatment, security and all. I wasn't her only submissive though, and that left space to be alone, mingle, and get to know others. I was walking in the hallway when I saw her. Not Big Mama . . . but the Colombian smurf. Why was she here? I ran into the first room I could get to frantically searching for Big Mama and luckily found her in a room and not occupied with anyone.

"Get her out of here, who invited her?" She demanded answers but more importantly, she insisted security keep watch on me the remainder of our time there. To be in a lifestyle where you are physically beaten, how could one feel so safe?

Big Mama indeed proved that it could be different. The rest of the weekend went well. I went home sore, but not afraid. Loved but confused and there was my shame. I thought I left it behind in New York.

It wasn't until a couple of years later that Jordan and I were in conversation and I told her of how I was out of that lifestyle for good, that I was finding my worth, and I didn't need to be beaten to know I was loved. There was One who took the punishment for me, and me trying to endure it myself just made His suffering in vain. I couldn't be responsible for that.

I am not sure if she heard what I actually said, or if she would accept it for her truth as well and come out of this lifestyle with me.

She did however inform me lightheartedly, "So how does it feel to be a porn star?"

"Now sis, you know good and well I never did anything sexual here. That's not what it was for me."

"Maybe not for you . . . but why do you think they recorded you at the event?"

My shame tried to flood over me like a tidal wave . . . but God. I knew this was my past, and while I felt so stupid, gullible, and naive . . . how could one be so naive? I reached out one last time to Big Mama and her crew and begged them to delete any and all footage and photos. I signed an agreement that it was all destroyed and could not be used. That, folks, is how you become an accidental porn star.

While I say that flippantly and with jest, this is a real life that so many are consumed in. Every one of them have their own story, their own reasoning for why they are there. What I realized is that I simply traded alcohol and self-harm for this lifestyle. It's an addiction—an addiction to pain that numbs the hurt within. It's a temporary fix. It's a bandaid to get you through for another week or so, and you'll find yourself assuming the position again, grabbing the bottle again, cutting/burning again, getting high again, recklessly spending your life savings again—whatever your addiction. I can promise you it is only a bandaid fix.

Think back to when it all started. Now think a little harder because I can assure you it started further back than your initial thought. If we want to feel whole, complete, secure, you must get to the root of the heartache.

> **Allow God to excavate the brokenness and mend it back together into something beautiful, something that will last much longer than just a week.**

Our marriage continued to have its ups and downs. I wrote most of it off as a typical marriage—just forgive and love him anyway. I wasn't perfect by any measure. My PTSD caused a lot of issues in the bedroom, as one could imagine. We worked through them. He was always patient and kind. I respected him so much for that, and

I kept finding myself falling back into his security. A year in, we found ourselves pregnant.

Ava was born in August 2015. We fought through our very different parenting styles. While he was the only dad Savannah had ever known, it just wasn't the same and it was very clear. As was now his second youngest, for me. Her circumstances were different, and her mom was in and out of her life after we married, making all of our lives a living hell. She ended up moving back with her mom, only making more evident the issues I was having with my husband were NOT with his daughter, rather truly between us.

In 2016, he left us. No text, call, email, not even a telegram. He was just gone. I didn't know what we would do. I was a stay-at-home mom at this time, and I spent all day praying, asking God to show me where he was or to at least bring him back. A week later he walked through the front door as if it was any other day after work, and I was left speechless. I wasn't angry; I wasn't happy. I struggled to find emotions or any words to even give him. I didn't get anything more than he had been sleeping in the church parking lot all week, went to work, grabbed dinner, and got to work early to wash up. Oh yeah, I most certainly had a lot of questions, a lot of doubt. But having him there gave us a security of home and family I had so desperately longed for, and even more so wanted for my girls.

In October 2016, we nearly lost Ava. She woke up one Friday afternoon from a nap and couldn't walk. I wrote it off as her foot was asleep, and at two years old, she could not express what she was feeling. An hour later though, her slow, assisted walk turned into a crawl. Then an army crawl into my arms, and she was burning up. Fever of 103. I did what mommas do: a little Tylenol, hydration, a quick trip to the doctor for some tests, and lots and lots of TLC.

The next day, we still didn't have results. Thankfully, her doctor's office was open on Saturdays for half a day, so I called and demanded some results. Her blood draws never made it to the lab. After a dozen apologies, they put a stat on her tests to get results. I was unable to control her fever, she was no longer mobile at all, and

I just heard my spirit say, "GO!" Before we had her fully buckled in, the doctor called and said, "Turn on your flashers and get her to the closest emergency room, don't stop for anything!" My heart sank, and fear quickly set in, but I had to be strong for my baby girl.

The hospital was waiting for us when we arrived and they took her straight back. Her fever was now 106.9, and the room was full of doctors and nurses. They continued to take her back and forth for every scan and test they could think of. It was during early morning rounds when we were told they would be rushing her in for emergency surgery within the hour. She had MRSA in her blood and developed a staph infection inside her bone; they would have to go in and clean it out. They warned me that she could be violent when waking up from anesthesia, but I assured them, this was the happiest girl they'd ever met, always full of joy and laughter. I choked on those words real quick. My once joyful child was acting as though she was possessed by demons and we could not control her. She ripped the IV out; one second she's hugging me, then she was trying to claw my eyes out. I felt so helpless, my heart shattered to see her this way in so much pain and confusion and I didn't know how to fix it. My husband stood at the foot of the bed and said, "I can't deal with this, I just can't" and walked out of the hospital.

Just like God to be steps ahead of us. This time He came in as a sweet friend of mine, Leslie. Sure, she had a phone and YouTube, but the peace that came over Ava and me was not from any cartoon on YouTube.

> **I knew while one father walked out, another Father walked into the room and said, "Peace, be still," and everything yielded to His command.**

We spent eight days in the hospital monitoring her numbers, started physical therapy, and prayed she would recover quickly. So many came to see her and brought gifts. We never felt so loved. We left that hospital with two red Radio Flyer wagons stuffed with gifts. Savannah bounced from one home to the next between friends. My heart ached so badly to see her in the evenings. She wasn't allowed in the room for a few days, nor was she able to see Ava. It took a toll on her sweet soul. But we found a way to make it all work. We were told that Ava would probably not walk for a month. "Don't rush it. Just let it happen."

A week before we were admitted into the hospital, we were in a thrift store and Ava wanted this Fisher Price shopping cart . . . $15! I just couldn't do it. I needed to get them clothes and we were not, as you would say, rolling in the dough. We were on a tight budget. On our way to our car, a lady came running out of the Little Angel thrift store yelling, "HEY! WAIT! I hope you don't mind but I had to get it for her, please take it as a gift. Be blessed." I was shocked and Ava . . . well, she was really happy!

The day we came home from the hospital, I laid her on the couch, got her comfy, and put Dory on for the 357th time. I went to the bathroom and came back into the room. Ava was WALKING! Go ahead . . . take a guess how she was walking . . . I'll wait. That's right . . . that ol' $15 Fisher Price shopping cart that was bought for her the week prior by a stranger at the Little Angel. WON'T GOD DO IT!

I didn't always see God in every circumstance while I was going through it, especially in my earlier years. There were times I questioned if He even cared, doubted that He could hear me, much less dwell with me in the frequent pits I found myself in. But I cannot tell my story without Him. I cannot tell this story and not see the evidence of God all over my life, regardless if I felt it at the time or not.

What about you? Does He dwell with you? Or are you in a season where you find yourself shaking your fist at the heavens demanding Him to show Himself? It's okay if you are, God can handle your anger. Ask Him to show you the video reel of your life and show you where He was in every season. Peace isn't the absence of struggle. It's the ability to have your very breath speak YAHWEH in the midst of it.

My marriage had its good times. We did our own camping trips and boating on Jordan Lake. We took our family to Myrtle Beach just as tradition would have it. Our girls were loved well and they knew it. It was in the sixth year of our marriage though that something went terribly awry. It took me a long time to figure it out. It had me so confused. I was drawing nearer to God and digging deeper than ever. God had even given me someone to help me navigate my PTSD, as my episodes began to flare up worse than ever and nearly left me dead on Vandora Springs Rd.

I went to a small group and I was triggered oddly in relation to my mother, not Mike. I panicked. I was humiliated and I just had to run. I sped away in my car going sixty-five miles per hour about to go into the roundabout. I had just enough clarity to call and communicate with the one helping me process PTSD that I was spiraling into an episode and I couldn't stop.

Blue lights. I was being pulled over. My friend was still on speaker.

"I am sorry, officer. I have PTSD and I am not sure where I am, but I am not where I think I am." I tried to explain through my sobbing.

I don't know what my friend said . . . I was just trying to count my breaths. That officer stayed with me until I came to the reality of where I was. He assured me that at my speed I wouldn't have made it home tonight.

"Go home. You're going to be okay."

No ticket was issued, he never even asked for my license and registration. Yeah, I give God credit for that one too. Still rescuing me all these years later.

The closer I drew to God, the further I got from my husband. He no longer joined us for church and seldom made a softball game to see the girls play. We barely spoke, much less had any physical affection of any sort. I found mail hidden that revealed debt and other secrets. What is done in secret will always be brought to the light sooner or later.

I was accused of an affair multiple times, with none other than my best friend's husband. It made no sense, and I began to pray for clarity.

Between church, helping our community, homeschooling the girls, coaching softball, and taking care of our home—complete with a garden—when in the world would I even have time for an affair? It bothered me because it questioned my integrity. It bothered me because why was God allowing this? Why wasn't He defending me now, when I had surrendered everything to Him? I did everything God asked me to, making myself vulnerable on a whole new level to save my marriage. NOTHING seemed to work.

I was so mad at God. God of the universe got me doing all these things, knowing good and well beforehand it's not going to work. But there was a spontaneous moment that gave me a glimpse of hope. We found ourselves in an intimate moment, and I felt this dreadful season was finally ending!

It didn't quite happen like that. I honestly didn't know if it was my PTSD or if God was giving me the answers I specifically asked him for. While the only evidence I have is what God spoke that day, I am convinced He had never lied to me before.

Through my tears, I questioned my husband. "What was that?" I asked.

He just blew me off and said "I don't know what you're talking about." He couldn't even look at me. It was the first time he was intentionally heartless toward me. I didn't know who the other woman was, but I know I asked for abundantly clear answers and God gave them. It had been a long time since I felt shame that deep. I just wanted to crawl in the shower and cry . . . and that's just what I did.

Over the next few months, I asked him to join me in counseling. I asked him point blank, and God told me to forgive him. While Jack never admitted to anything, even to this day, I told him I forgave him and we could work through this. Three times we had these conversations on that front porch. Three times he refused. Join us back at church and get counseling, both together and individually. God was giving us a game plan complete with special date nights that I knew would heal the brokenness between us. And God said, "GO."

Me, My Girls, & Jesus

While my Baptist roots were so confused as to why God was telling me to leave my marriage, and I was freaking out and had so many questions, there was that indescribable peace that surpassed all understanding. I knew that as deep as I had gone with Him already, He had only begun to scratch the surface. He didn't answer all of my questions; He just gave me my next step.

> **What an honor that the God of the universe would see me, know me, and love me so deeply that He would walk each and every step with me.**

It wasn't until 2021 that I realized I never really trusted Him before. Oh, I loved Him, I knew He was faithful, I knew He was good . . . but I only trusted Him when I had the space to control part of the outcome as well.

I was a stay-at-home, homeschooling mama and had been out of the workforce for years. Flipping burgers was not going to sustain us anymore. I put in some applications and God said start packing. So I did. I literally found myself not doing a single move without His next instruction. While it wouldn't have been rocket science to figure out what to do, I was learning a new meaning to submission—submission to His Spirit. It was a beautiful process and still is!

It wasn't long before I found myself stranded in the Dollar General yet again because my card had been declined. This was the third time in our marriage that I was cut off from our finances, to feel the humiliation and finding ways to defend him to our girls. He isn't a bad man, just deeply broken. I had opened my own bank account a few years prior when he last cut me off and vowed to not have that happen again, so thankfully, I was at least able to leave the store with what we came for.

I got a job with 2u2day Logistics delivering for Amazon. It truly was a work of God that I passed the driving portion of the test.

Please love your delivery driver and show them grace on the road. You don't understand the blind spots and toll that job takes on the body until you live a day in the life. They worked with me way more than I ever expected them to. I didn't share this with my husband. I didn't need to. Our relationship was over and we were in transition to our next season.

I took care of the girls and had a tribe of people helping me care for them during this season. Nonetheless, I knew he'd eventually find out. When he did, I just let him spew it out. I'd never been so hurt by his words. While I knew they were not my truth, it still made me feel like I was neglecting my girls, and I felt guilty to have to leave them especially during this time of uncertainty. While they were hurting, confused, and felt the tension in the house, they too had this peace within them that just couldn't be explained.

God gave me another job with someone at our church, answering phones and scheduling appointments for his RV repair company. 2u2day Logistics was gracious and let me go ahead and leave rather than waiting two weeks given my circumstances. I will be forever grateful for 2u2day Logistics for their grace and compassion they had for me and my girls.

I applied for so many apartments and single-family homes to rent as I was not in the position to buy. Regardless of how honest I was about my situation before filling out applications, my money was taken left and right. It was so frustrating.

I laughed and said, "No way I can afford that place nor would I qualify," when God led me to an apartment complex in Apex. Another family from our church, the Snyders, supported me and the girls in every way in this season. They were frustrated with the process we were enduring and even spoke with the apartment manager beforehand. They offered to cosign. The apartment manager assured us that, in the worst-case scenario, I'd have to have them cosign for me. They guaranteed to get me in, but they explained that they'd have to deny me first and do it the right way.

So, I filled out the application, already exhaling, knowing at least this would be taken care of. I just waited for their call back to deny me. The phone rang, and before I could say hello, God said, "Watch this . . ."

"Hello, Mrs.Parton . . . you're approved." I didn't even hear them. I was asking for instructions on what the Snyders needed to do. They repeated it a few times more before it clicked, and I said, "But how?"

BUT GOD!

We set the move date. While I wanted to let the girls enjoy their Christmas where they were, Jack was rushing us out because he had family coming into town and didn't want me there. So, on December 17, 2021, we moved to Apex. While we thanked God and celebrated His faithfulness, there was still a grieving process that had to happen.

In August of that year, God called Mama LeeLee home. I'd never been so devastated. While I loved her deeper than most on this side of heaven, I couldn't have been prepared for the grieving I went through after losing her. Just a couple of weeks before we moved, Savannah lost her emotional support dog, Conner. He was a special boy. We also lost Lee Rouse (Pops), Papa Parton, Max Tudor (my best friend's son, who so graciously donated his Friday morning to help us move), Grandma Alice, and Grandpa Dick. Our church closed in October 2021, and the girls and I were losing the house where we created a home. All of these losses occurred between August 2021 and February 2022.

Our hearts still grieve for everyone we lost during those years. The time hit so quickly and suddenly that we never had the time to grieve one before someone else passed. They knocked the wind out of us, leaving us with unanswered questions and a shaken faith.

We navigated the tidal waves of grief, leaning on each other and into our Father's chest. Despite feeling angry, confused, and hurt, we couldn't deny that He was in the middle of it all. We didn't know how He would turn all that loss for good, but we believed Him for it.

In August 2022, as my grief welled up for Mama LeeLee, there was a new grief about to hit. My boss went radio silent; nearly four hours passed before I got word from his wife that he had a massive heart attack. He had been revived but wasn't out of the woods yet. He had to undergo many procedures and surgeries and was not able to return to work as strong as he once was, meaning, I suddenly lost my job.

So, God moves me, takes my church, takes my Mama, takes my job . . . what now God? I was scared. As a single mama with two girls solely depending upon me to take care of them, it had been nearly two months since my last paycheck. Thankfully, I had money in savings, so we were okay, but I was getting really concerned.

I wanted to keep the girls homeschooled and finding a legit work-from-home job was far and few between, and let's not discuss my qualifications. I blamed God for taking so much from me, so many valuable assets in my life. Yet, He also had already started moving people into my life, including Elevation Church, to get me through this next season.

He gave me dreams and instructions to share my story with the pastor's wife. How do you tell the pastor's wife that you were an "accidental porn star?" I was not ready, but this was a new phase in life and I owed Him everything at this point. He'd proven His faithfulness to me; I would do the same.

So, we set it up for the ungodly hour of 5:00 am to "walk and talk" in a park. I left some shame in those woods that morning I wasn't even aware I was still carrying. I was worried some of my story would push her away, that I'd be judged or she'd try to deliver me from all iniquities that should remain.

Nope. She had questions alright; we found ourselves able to laugh a bit through it, and there was nothing but love from her. We exchanged phone numbers, and she invited me to join her small group, although I specifically said "I am not looking to join one at this time." Some call it stubbornness, but I knew it was obedience to what the Spirit was telling her. This was not your typical pastor's wife. I quickly realized she was a fierce warrior for the Kingdom of God and she won't back down!

She's the real deal, full of compassion and grace; yet, she will also challenge you to rise up to the next level. Being around her, you find yourself better just by her presence. Such people are rare in this world. God had truly given me a treasured gift in her. I wasn't sure if she'd remember my name, but I would never forget hers or what she did for me that morning.

On October 23, 2022, I missed church due to all three of us having a stomach virus of some sort. I received a text from her that someone had just walked in and asked if she knew anyone looking for a job and didn't mind working from home.

That was it! Did she remember my name? Did she tell him my name? What was happening? It's funny how God will remove you from situations when you have control issues, and He just wants you to let Him be God and do what He does best.

She finally texted back the next day connecting us, and I had an interview that morning. Praying God would keep all bodily fluids inside for thirty minutes so I could get through this interview, I was very honest. I had no idea anything about his industry but with a lil grace and patience, I would do whatever it took to learn, and I would always have his back.

I started as the Operations Manager of a locally-owned publishing and marketing company on October 31, 2022. It was a monumental learning experience and interesting to work with people who were located near and also halfway around the globe. While that season didn't last as long as I would have liked it to, I met some incredible people. I got to hear their stories, meet their beautiful families, even those living across the world that I thankfully still have the privilege of staying in contact with.

Single motherhood isn't easy for me. It presents challenges that humble one real quick. I lean on my church family to get me through the hard days and hear the echoes of guidance from Mama LeeLee. I pray often that I can be at least half the mom she was for me to my girls. In June, I'll celebrate eight years of sobriety from self-harm and alcoholism, and I couldn't be more proud of myself. It hasn't been easy; the temptation still rears its ugly head. But that's when I turn to my eGroup (my small group Bible study), that I hadn't wanted in the beginning. But God knew what I'd need.

We're not meant to do life alone.

While there are real people behind those lit screens (whether phone, tablet, or computer), it never compares to making ourselves vulnerable to the glory of God so He can physically wrap His broad, loving arms around us.

Savannah, now fourteen, and Ava, now nine, have both defied the odds—not by their own might but by the strength of their Father within them. We're a devoted softball family. Savannah aspires to play for Campbell University while pursuing a career in early childhood education. Meanwhile, Ava dreams of becoming a professional basketball player, aiming to join any team with purple uniforms. Both continue to excel at Parton Academy, testing above their grade level. Oh yeah, their future is bright!

I became a first-time homeowner in April and I can't wait to build a new garden! I am anxious to start sowing seeds in my garden while, in parallel, I am confident God will use my story to sow seeds of hope and endurance in your life. Wouldn't it be just like God to give me a story full of His glory and evidence of His faithfulness and then perfectly position me with a publishing company that led to lifelong friendships? You'd think that He had it all figured out . . . way back in the spring of '98.

- CHAPTER 13 -

Glory in My Story

Hold up! I bet you thought it was over, didn't you? Well, there's one last bit to my story—so far—that must be told.

I mentioned we lost Grandma Alice and Grandpa Dick in 2021-2022. They are Savannah's paternal grandparents, and unfortunately, they only got to hold her a couple of times. I was surprised at just how hard their passing hit her. While we spoke every week (less frequent when their health declined), I guess I never realized how important those phone calls were to her as well.

They were unaware of our life in Minnesota. I couldn't bring myself to tell them. We agreed that what was said between us would remain private, and we wouldn't discuss Mike. Although we bent the rules a couple of times for special reasons, we kept it brief and avoided discussing past events. They were some of my biggest supporters raising Savannah.

Alice, a retired school teacher, initially had doubts when I chose to homeschool. However, I was moved to tears many times when she expressed how proud she was. She could see that I was doing the right things for Savannah and Ava. Oh yeah, they adopted Ava right on into their family as well. Each year, they sent Christmas ornaments symbolizing that year, and we continue this tradition in their memory. They will forever be deeply loved by all of us and hold a special place in our hearts.

When they passed, I received a phone call from their phone. It was Mary, one of Mike's sisters. We had never spoken other than the couple of times we met in person nearly thirteen years ago. She explained how, going through her parents' belongings and their messages, she could see we truly loved and cared for each other, and she was sorry she didn't try to reach out sooner. I'd always wondered why . . . but it was very complicated circumstances, and I am sure everyone had questions we were too afraid to ask.

Mary and I started building a relationship. Savannah? Well, it took her a little time to warm up and trust her. All she knows of her father is that he is not a safe man, and she didn't know what to expect from the rest of the family.

That year, Mary and her husband Scott sent us Christmas gifts, and they were such thoughtful gifts. They also adopted Ava in as their niece.

Word did get out to one of her best friends—her little sister Colleen, despite my trust in Mary to keep the agreement I had with her parents—that we leave Mike out of our conversations. I don't want him knowing anything about us or where we live. From what I remembered, Colleen always scared me a bit. She was the baby of the family (five kids), and I always believed she had the most questions that were right on the tip of her tongue, but they were never asked. I don't blame her. Mike was pretty toxic and foul to his family. It was always one of our biggest arguments, me defending his parents. I became anxious when Mary told me that Colleen wanted in too. I was worried that if more of them knew, sooner or later Mike would find out and start trouble again.

On June 16, 2023, we picked up a rental and headed for Williamsburg, Virginia. This is where Colleen now resides with the love of her life, James. It was Savannah's curiosity that gave me the courage to go. I was so anxious I got a speeding ticket just twenty minutes down the road. My mind was spinning, and I was nauseous at the thoughts. Yet, Savannah and Ava were as cool as cucumbers. At least until we pulled in on the cobblestone road that led us to some really cute shops.

We sat in the car for what seemed like hours. My paranoia was on high alert. I was looking for his storm chaser truck or anyone who looked suspicious and might try to attack us, already in tears before I even opened the door. Three and a half hours on the road and I didn't know if I could even get out. We took our time. I didn't know where they would be. God help us if they came up from behind us.

I saw Scott and Mary first. They really hadn't changed a bit. Colleen and James were behind them, under this big tree. All I could think was: what if "he" was behind it, waiting to come for Savannah? Mary asked, "Please, can I hug you, is it okay?" She was like a kid on Christmas morning. She couldn't contain herself, and I didn't have the heart to tell her no. I wasn't sure when she would let go, but I think the longer we stayed in her embrace, the more peace set in.

Colleen, James, Scott . . . they all approached with caution and respected the circumstances. They wanted nothing more than to make us feel safe. They didn't know the story; they could only imagine, more so now, seeing my posture firsthand.

We ate at Mellow Mushroom. I don't know if they planned ahead to reserve a table outside, knowing it would make me more comfortable, or if that was God smiling down on me. I struggled to eat; it was all I could do to simply breathe. I asked them if I could share my story with them. It was the first time that anyone in his family knew why or how I ended up in Minnesota and what truly happened that kept me there. They apologized over and over again, and while I waited a long time for an apology for the hell we went through, it shouldn't have come from them. Yet, it still brought healing I didn't expect.

I still remember trying to put my pizza in a box to take home, my hands shaking uncontrollably. Colleen looked at me. Actually looked AT me, not through me, or around me. Despite what I had shared and my brokenness now exposed, she said, "Hun, let me help you with that." Piece by piece, God started assuring me that we were okay, we were safe.

We went into shops, and they made up for the years of spoiling they had missed out on. Then, we were invited to the home of Colleen and James. Being our first time meeting and my PTSD, I thought it best for the girls and me to stay in our own place. I never expected to go to their home. Things definitely felt more vulnerable, but we also started to feel like family—a family the girls had never had the chance to really experience as far as aunts and uncles. They were loving every minute of it.

Savannah and I were ushered upstairs to see the memorial for their parents, while Ava stayed downstairs coloring with her new uncles. Mary shared some stories of how she would visit and see the girls' pictures on their fridge, and how she'd watched them grow over the years in that way.

As Mary went back downstairs and Savannah followed, I grieved for the first time for my friends. They were in-laws, but even though I didn't want to be married, they became family. And afterwards, we truly became best friends. I cried for what seemed like an hour. Deep grieving happened upstairs, and I prayed they wouldn't hear my sobbing.

We shared dinner together that night—Pike Tacos! It had been a while, but it brought a flood of memories back of their mom in the kitchen; no one would ever leave her home hungry. Ava connected with Colleen, adding ketchup to her tacos. I still disapprove of ketchup on tacos, but it does make me smile to think of the connection we ALL had found.

We exchanged stories and leaned on each other for healing. The next day, we visited with them, nearly all day—between walking the historic town, lounging by the pool, and another dinner together. We played putt-putt in the rain, and Savannah saw a glimpse of true love between the "newlyweds"—Colleen and James. I believe it's actually been a few years now, but they're still head over heels for one another. It inspired her, and she now has them as her relationship goals.

While Aunt Mary is the softer one, Savannah learned that Aunt Colleen is so much like her. Savannah may be my twin, but when it comes to personality, she is her Aunt Colleen through and through. Uncle Scott and Uncle James were a toss-up as to who was more fun and who could make the best dad jokes. I was surprised to see how quickly both girls took to them, as they don't typically gravitate toward men.

The house was filled with giggles; there was a spark in their eyes—there was hope. Hope that they may have found their family in the most unexpected places.

> **I waited fifteen years for God to turn my story for good. I doubted it. How could good ever come from such a dark place?**

I now battle with PTSD, and it's so frustrating at times because it's so unexpected. One minute you are fine, and the next you find yourself spiraling and grasping for anything that will anchor you to reality. How could any good come from that?

It's okay to doubt. God isn't surprised by your doubt. He can handle your anger and forgive your unbelief, despite His consistent faithfulness. Give yourself a little grace and just rest in His promises. It may take fifteen years, it could take even longer . . . but I promise you, He is faithful to see it through! There is glory in your story also. Stay the course. Lean in. At times, the waiting seems to be endless, but God is a God of intricate details, and He will not do His grand reveal until His perfect timing.

If you find yourself reading this and you're still waiting for God to turn your story into His glory . . . hang tight. It's on its way!

(Left to right) James, Colleen, Scott, Mary, Ava, Savannah, myself

GRATITUDE

To everyone that ever spoke life over me . . . know that your echoes of truth pushed me through my darkest nights. The seeds you planted, now bear fruit. Your embrace was an extension of my Father's love for me and I will never forget the impact you had on my life.

IN LOVING MEMORY

Mama LeeLee

September 7, 1970 ~ August 1, 2021

To my beautiful girls,

I fought battles and have overcome generational curses so you wouldn't have to carry the burden or endure any more hardships than you need to. Hardships are guaranteed on this side of heaven. Don't be afraid of them.

Remember the story from Mrs. Lori and her time in Africa. How the people, even as young children, would hear the roar of the lion and would have to run at it to attack in order to protect their village. Run into the roar. Do it afraid, and remember you yourselves are bold lionesses!

Remember, there will be days you will fail, but you are courageous enough to rise again. Without the challenging seasons, you will become complacent and distant from the Father's heart.

Remember who you are and to whom you belong. You are deeply loved and fully known, and God has a distinct purpose for your life that only you can fulfill.

You are Chosen.
You are Beautiful.
You are Loved.
You are Redeemed.
You are Kind.
You are Bold.
You are Called.
You are Brave.
You are Forgiven.
You are an Overcomer.
You are His Beloved.

My prayer for you is that you always remember that while some battles require you to run into the roar, some will require you to surrender—not in defeat, but to your Father. On your knees, hands high, and hearts abandoned in praise. Never allow your confidence to keep you from being humble. He's in it with you, fighting for you!

Even when you find yourself angry, confused, frustrated, isolated, or weary...praise Him! Look at your Father's track record... He is faithful! If you can't see it for yourself, ask Him to show you His hand in every season of your life. Trust that your Father will always have your best interest at the center of His heart. He will never leave you nor forsake you. He sees you and looks at you with great delight!

Rise up, beautiful girls! Rise up, lift your head, and know you are a child of the most high God!

All my love,

Mom

YOU ARE NOT ALONE.
HELP IS HERE.

Not everyone has a strong community or support system, but there's always a starting point for help. If you or someone you know is experiencing domestic violence, there's a place to turn.

Your safety and well-being matter.

National Domestic Violence Hotline:
1-800-799-SAFE (7233)

HEALING STARTS WITH A SINGLE STEP.

Trauma can leave deep scars, but no one has to go through it alone. Whether your path is just beginning or you've been struggling in silence, there's help waiting for you.

PTSD doesn't define you—seeking support can change your life.

PTSD Helpline:
1-800-273-8255 (Press 1 for Veterans)

YOUR LIFE MATTERS.

National Suicide & Crisis Lifeline:
Call or Text 988 for immediate help

FIND FREEDOM
FIND COMMUNITY

Celebrate Recovery is a safe place to find freedom from your hurts, hang-ups, and habits.

www.celebraterecovery.com

Let's bring your story to life.